My obaachan (grandmother), Misako Kameda
(1928–2006)

This book is an ode to the everyday meals that you find in the homes of the mothers and grandmothers of Japan. It is the food that I grew up with, the food that I get nostalgic for and the food I like to make my family when we need nourishment.

For my ancestors and
my children.

EMIKO DAVIES

MEMORIES
AND
STORIES FROM
MY FAMILY'S
KITCHEN

GOHAN

ごはん

Smith
Street
Books

INTRODUCTION 7

一

HOME-MADE
PANTRY STAPLES

26

二

JAPANESE
BREAKFAST

38

三

RICE

74

四

VEGETABLES

110

五

NOODLES &
STREET FOOD

144

六

FAMILY
FAVOURITES

170

七

THE WEST MEETS JAPAN

204

八

SWEETS

228

Gohan literally means 'rice' in Japanese – and when I think of this word, I think quite specifically about a small ceramic bowl of fragrant, glistening, steamed, slightly sticky rice. Tellingly, it is also the general word for a 'family meal'. A bowl of rice is what most home-cooked Japanese meals revolve around. It's there for asagohan (breakfast) with a bowl of miso soup, some pickles, tofu and a piece of grilled fish. It's soaking up the sauce in a comforting donburi bowl, or wrapped in nori in the ultimate hirugohan (portable lunch), onigiri. And it's there for bangohan (dinner), perhaps served with a pickled plum, with a mild Japanese curry or a flavourful braised fish.

If you haven't eaten rice, you haven't eaten. I can still hear Obaachan, my Japanese grandmother, announcing that dinner is ready with, 'Gohan desuyo!'

—

My grandparents, Misako and Chodo, both from southern Japan, were the long-standing custodians of a temple – my grandfather became a Buddhist priest after the Second World War – and the house attached to it in a small town in Chiba prefecture, not far from Tokyo. The house was serene, all wood and paper screens, with a garden pond full of colourful, patterned and rather boisterous koi fish, manicured bonsai and a huge persimmon tree that in winter was laden with heavy fruit. The next-door neighbours sold eggs and their large flock of chickens provided an endless chorus of clucking and crowing that could be heard at all hours of the day and night, which I grew very fond of – I am still taken back to that house when I hear roosters crowing at random hours of the day.

Growing up, I moved with my family from Australia to China, back and forth, twice, by the time I was eleven years old, eventually spending eight years in China until I finished high school and then I went even further away to college, in Rhode Island on the east coast of the United States. I moved to Florence several years after graduating, in 2005, and have called Italy home ever since. Through all this moving around, my grandparents' temple remained the one constant home base in my life, the place to which I would return every single year to spend my holidays. Although I haven't been back to that house since my grandparents passed away when I was twenty-six, if I just close my eyes, I can still feel the temple's tatami floors underneath my bare feet and the

'IF YOU HAVEN'T EATEN RICE, YOU HAVEN'T EATEN!'

7

weight of the tall, dimpled water glasses in my hands. I can feel the hot water coming right up to my chin in the deep bathtub and I can hear the trickle of hot tea coming out of the thermos that stood, fixed, on the table for anyone who needed a reviving sip of hojicha (roasted green tea). But most of all I can remember the smell of Obaachan's cooking, wafting out from behind the swinging, saloon-style doors that separated the dining room from her kitchen: a mixture of her freshly steamed rice, salted dried fish and vegetables braising sweetly in dashi.

My obaachan made the best food, full stop. It was something I looked forward to every single visit. It wasn't shojin ryori, the restrained, almost-vegan temple cuisine of Zen Buddhists; hers was proper home cooking and, in line with the flexitarian philosophy of their Buddhist sect, it consisted mostly of vegetables and plenty of tofu, but also fish and eggs, with the occasional beef sukiyaki (undeniably her signature dish) for special occasions, such as when we would visit. The recipes in this book reflect this, with many options and suggestions for making most of these dishes suitable for vegetarians, too.

Obaachan cooked with care and used food like medicine. In fact, she had a huge dislike of Western medicine and preferred looking after herself by eating well. Freshly arrived off a long flight, or tired from a long, hot day in a steamy Japanese summer, she would offer her home-made pickles as a pick-me-up – 'vinegar is good for your tired body', she would say. Tea or miso soup made a remedy for most things and eating grilled isobe mochi could keep you warm for hours on a cold winter's day.

This book is all of these things, and more – the everyday meals that you find in the homes of the mothers and grandmothers of Japan, rather than in restaurants. It is the food that I grew up with, the food that I get nostalgic for and that I still request my mother to make whenever I get a chance. It is the food I like to make my family whenever we need nourishment but I don't have a lot of time to cook, because (unlike what many people think) Japanese home cooking is not fiddly, or time-consuming – it's quick and remarkably simple, thanks to the Japanese philosophy that good, fresh, seasonal food doesn't need much to enhance its natural flavour and shouldn't be overcooked.

When I asked my mother, Sumie, what she thought about the idea of calling a book on Japanese home cooking 'Gohan', she said to me, 'Gohan means the everyday home-cooked meal. Nothing fussy, but quick and easy, and nourishing. One that is made with love. I think the best food is created when you cook for someone you love.' She paused and reminded me of a drawing my eldest daughter Mariù did when she was five, before she could write properly. It's a recipe for soup, where all the ingredients are drawn instead of written. One of the ingredients is a heart. 'Remember Mariù's soup recipe that had love as an ingredient?' she asked. 'To me that is "Gohan".' ●

My mother Sumie, my grandmother Misako, my aunt Yukiko and me.

'Gohan to me means the everyday home-cooked meal. Nothing fussy, but quick and easy, and nourishing. One that is made with love. I think the best food is created when you cook for someone you love.'

MY MOTHER
SUMIE

澄
江

ITADAKIMASU: MORE THAN JUST 'BON APPÉTIT'

頂きます

10

Itadakimasu (頂きます) literally means 'to receive', 'to get' or 'accept'. I think it is best described as language researcher Mami Suzuki says, '"I humbly receive," but in a mealtime setting, it's compared to "let's eat", "bon appétit", or "thanks for the food". Some even liken it to the religious tradition of saying grace before eating.'

The roots of this word date back to the beginning of Buddhism in Japan – the kanji at the start of the word (頂) originally meant 'mountaintop', or 'over one's head' (imagine putting your hands above your head in the shape of a mountain peak – this gesture, with a bow, was the literal acting out of this kanji character when receiving food or gifts from someone of higher status in Buddhism and it came to mean 'to receive'). Itadakimasu is also a reflection of the Buddhist concept to thank nature for nourishing your life. It is a way of thanking not only who cooked the meal, but also who grew, harvested, made or hunted your food, even the plants, fish and animals. It is a sign of respect for all the living things that created the meal, so even if you made the meal yourself, you are still giving thanks.

In another literal sense of the phrase, which puts all this into perspective, it can mean 'I receive the lives of animals and plants for my own life.'

My mother, Sumie, always taught us this concept and it was instilled in me as a young adolescent when she took me and my siblings on a holiday into the mountains of Nikko. We stayed in a beautiful, traditional ryokan (inn) by a lake and one day we were served the freshest sashimi made of fish caught from the lake. To show how fresh it was, in fact, the chef had artfully sliced the sashimi and arranged it on a handmade plate with the fish's carcass – the head, tail and backbone, still intact and attached together – as the garnish. Although the fish was no longer alive, it clearly had been until just moments before, so the head and tail were still moving. We children were mortified – my little sister burst into tears (she has in fact been a vegetarian for most of her life). My mother quickly asked if the chef could rearrange the sashimi without the moving features and it was brought out again on a different plate, in a new way with different garnishes. I looked at it hesitantly, but my mother just said to me gently, 'We should honour it – this fish gave its life for us for our lunch.' To not eat it would be a terrible waste. I thanked the fish, the chef and my mother with 'itadakimasu' before enjoying that lunch.

While this was practised in Buddhism for centuries, it wasn't until the 19th century that it became a national custom to say 'itadakimasu' before every meal. In 1812, a Japanese book of etiquette instructs when picking up chopsticks to thank all of nature, the emperor and your parents. Not long afterwards, this entire phrase was copied in schools, ending with 'itadakimasu'.

You say it before a meal, before picking up your chopsticks. You can bow your head slightly, put your hands together in prayer (although these two things are optional, depending on the circumstance) and say clearly, itadakimasu (pronounced *ee-tada-ki-mas*, with an ending like in 'Christmas').

While itadakimasu is said at the beginning of the meal, there is also a phrase to say at the very end before you get up from the table: *gochisosama* (ご馳走さま or *gochisosamadeshita* in polite form), which literally means, 'It was a great deal of work to prepare that meal,' acknowledging how much effort goes into putting food on the table – the 'chiso' part of the phrase means running around in a great effort, as in going all over the place to get the ingredients, not to mention the whole preparation of the meal – and can be interpreted as: 'Thank you for the meal – that was a feast.' These are words to say in the comfort of your own home with your family, as well as when dining in other people's homes or even dining out – you can say this to the chefs if it is an open kitchen or just casually as you leave a restaurant and it will always be appreciated. The Japanese-British-Australian author Katherine Tamiko Arguile puts it so perfectly in her book *Meshi*, 'Not saying these words before and after eating feels as unnatural as taking leave of a loved one without saying goodbye.' ●

SOMETHING FROM THE SEA, SOMETHING FROM THE MOUNTAIN

海
の
幸
と
山
の
幸

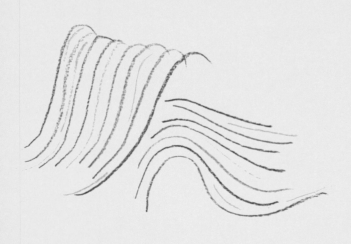

Japan is the fourth-largest island nation in the world, made up of almost 7,000 islands and nearly 30,000 kilometres of coastline. Of this land, about three-quarters of it is comprised of mountains, many of them volcanoes, with long ranges running down the archipelago like a spine.

My mother would say that the ideal Japanese meal should have both something from the sea and something from the mountain, or *umi no sachi yama no sachi* (海の幸と山の幸). *Sachi* means 'produce' or 'harvest', but the character itself (the one you see on the end of the phrase in Japanese) has a double meaning – on its own it also means 'happiness', so it could also be read as 'gifts from the sea, gifts from the mountain'.

What is so telling about this concept is not only a sense of gratefulness and respect for these 'gifts', but also how the landscape is so connected with what the Japanese eat, and this is something that I think also stretches further – it is not just the surrounding landscape and the traditions that come with that landscape, what you have available around you, but also the climate, the seasons, even the microseasons, and how the weather influences what you feel like eating.

Each season has its special ingredients, whether it's fish or mushrooms, fruit or nuts, but also changes in weather. Food can help you cope with the climate and eating becomes an extra joy, a comfort. In the very hot, humid Japanese summers, for example, it's common to eat chilled foods – noodle dishes become cold versions (my mother even serves her Cold somen noodles [page 158] with ice cubes), dishes like Nanbanzuke (page 191), marinated in vinegar (so they keep well), are enjoyed cold and there are many refreshing desserts and sweets to keep you going throughout the warm afternoons – jelly-like Kanten (page 253); Anmitsu (page 238), which is often served with ice cream, kanten and fresh fruit; even kakigori, which is a giant pile of flavoured shaved ice. And in the freezing-cold winters, there are endless, satisfying and nutritious hot soups, broths and stews, such as Oden (page 183) to warm you from the inside. ●

A BRIEF HISTORY
OF JAPANESE CUISINE:
ANCIENT RICE,
MEDIEVAL MONKS,
PORTUGUESE TRADERS
AND ISOLATION

和
食
の
歴
史

Many of the things you see in Japanese cuisine are incredibly ancient and virtually unchanged over the centuries. Rice is thought to have been introduced to Japan via Korea and China in the neolithic Yayoi period (around 400 BCE to 200 CE), although recent dating of the remnants of earthenware pots suggests it could have been centuries earlier, around 800 BCE. Japan has the perfect climate for wet-farming rice and in very little time it became a staple. This was also the period where the country became an agricultural society, 'the era of agricultural revolution', as Nancy Singleton Hachisu calls it in her book *Japan: The Cookbook*, borrowing other important crops like wheat, soybeans and adzuki beans from China and Korea, too, along with fruit like peaches and melons. These are all ingredients that make me think of Japanese cuisine.

Tofu-making, a practice brought from China by Zen Buddhist monks, and eating with chopsticks date back to the 8th century. Green tea was introduced in the 10th century. The suribachi, a textured bowl used for grinding, Japan's answer to the mortar and pestle, dates to the medieval Kamakura period.

Wheat noodles, like somen and udon, were the first noodles to appear in Japan in the mid-1300s, then came soba in the next century, thanks to advanced woodworking skills for good boards and rolling pins. Mochi and miso soup also date to this time, the Muromachi period (1336–1573). It is a period where, like the Italian Renaissance that was unfolding in Florence around the same time, the arts (in particular, theatre and ceramics) were also flourishing, alongside farming and world trade – as they did in Europe, New-World ingredients, such as chillies, sweet potatoes and pumpkin (winter squash), also arrived in Japan at this time.

The Muromachi period is also when, in 1543, the very first Europeans arrived in Japan in the form of Portuguese explorers and traders, and an important period of exchange, known as the Nanban Trade (literally 'southern barbarian' trade), began. The first Portuguese trades involved forbidden, sought-after silk that the Portuguese had picked up in China in exchange for highly prized, intricate Japanese silver. The cultural exchange that unfolded over this period led to many Portuguese influences in Japan, including language, weaponry, typography, religion and, naturally, gastronomy.

Many beloved Japanese dishes have their origins in this contact with the Portuguese and if you listen well you can hear it in some of the language: frying vegetables in a batter, otherwise known as tempura, comes from the Latin *quatuor tempora*, or simply *temporas* in Portuguese, referring to the quarterly periods of prayer in Christian churches when fasting and abstaining from meat would be observed. *Pan* meaning 'bread' and *panko* for 'breadcrumbs' (*ko* meaning 'flour'), and the resulting crumbed delights like crunchy korokke (croquettes), kasutera (like castella or pound cake), or nanbanzuke (escabeche) – the recipe for frying floured fish and preserving it in a vinegar dressing which literally translates to 'southern barbarian marinade' – as well as konpeito sweets (which comes from *confeito*, or *comfit*).

By the 1600s, Japan had entered into the Edo period, and shortly afterwards a decree of national isolation, called Sakoku, was declared, in part spurred on by the fear of colonialism and the rise of Christianity brought to the country by Portuguese missionaries. It lasted for 265 years, between 1603 and 1868. Over these centuries, almost all foreigners were banned from entering Japan and the Japanese from leaving the country, although there was still some selective trade with the Dutch, Chinese and Koreans. It ended when the US Navy sailed into the Bay of Edo with four impressive warships in 1853, forcing Japan to reopen.

While Japan turned inwards, however, trade among the previously separate local regions opened up and some of the most important ingredients in today's cuisine were developed and perfected: sake, soy sauce, vinegar, mirin and dashi, for example, as well as the practices of kaiseki ryori, the traditional multiple-course meal, and the Japanese tea ceremony. With these ceremonial events, the making of Japanese lacquerware, glass and ceramics to present the food and drinks beautifully on the table flourished as well.

THE 1,200-YEAR-OLD QUESTION OF MEAT

Buddhism was introduced to Japan during the Kofun period (300–538) and, as this new religion grew, so did the teachings of respect for life and that humans can be reincarnated into other creatures, in particular mammals – by killing an animal you may unknowingly be killing a reincarnated ancestor. Prior to this period, hunting wild forest animals like deer and boar was quite common and it supplemented the usual seafood diet, but as there was so little farming land and farm animals were used for work, meat wasn't a major source of protein. 'Protein was ingested from rice rather than from meat or milk,' writes historian Naomichi Ishige.

Author Zenjiro Watanabe paints this picture: 'The fact that rice is the staple of the Japanese diet was in fact dictated by nature and the Japanese climate. Moreover, the islands of Japan are blessed with abundant marine resources. With no need for meat, a community with a diet of rice and fish was born.'

In 675 came the official prohibition by Emperor Tenmu, banning the killing of animals (in line with both Buddhism and Japan's native Shintoism) and the eating of meat as a way to protect domestic livestock (cows, horses, dogs, chickens) that were needed for agricultural purposes; even monkeys were added to this list. The ban did not, however, include hunted wild birds and animals, but over the centuries even these were banned when the prohibition was reinforced by subsequent leaders.

There were some exceptions, though, namely fish and sea creatures (which were not banned in Shintoism), birds (which are sacred in Shintoism, but more acceptable as a food in Buddhism) and even hunted red meat was occasionally consumed in the form of 'medicine'. But meat remained a rarity and, if it did appear, it was done very privately and only in the very top tiers of society – there are numerous accounts of gifts being sent to Emperors in the form of meat or milk.

By the medieval Kamakura period, more and stricter orders against eating meat arrived. As author Zenjiro Watanabe describes, 'The order from Ise Shrine demanded a fast of one hundred days for eating the meat of domestic or wild animals. Further, anyone who ate with someone who consumed meat was ordered to fast for twenty-one days, while anyone who ate with someone who ate with someone else who consumed meat was ordered to fast for seven days.'

The reinforcement of these strict orders suggests that the ban against meat-eating had likely often been broken. Wild game and birds particularly were a frequent part of the diet despite the ban. In a country that is three-quarters mountains covered in lush, thick forest, wild animals abound and farmers were in a constant battle to keep their crops safe. Hunters would often sell their catch to markets in the city, where wild animal meat was considered medicinal, with restorative powers.

But abstaining from meat-eating was largely followed by the public and had become the way of life over the centuries. Hunters and fishermen and even restaurant owners would hold memorial services for the animals they killed. Even now, I can still remember my grandfather, a Buddhist priest, holding special prayers on behalf of the local chicken-shop owner who would come to mourn the lives of the animals.

When the Edo period ended, and Emperor Meiji came into power in 1868, there was a move to adopt Western practices and, for the Emperor, ending the meat ban was instrumental in moving forward. Four years later, the Emperor himself broke the nation's 1,200-year-old taboo and publicly ate meat to ring in the new year. It was a very difficult transition for the country, not only for devout Buddhists, to let go of such a deeply rooted custom and many anti-meat-eating movements arose, including an attack on the Emperor by Buddhist monks, which ended in four of them being shot. The Emperor then released this declaration to settle the matter once and for all: 'Although beef is a wonderfully nutritious food, there are still a great number of people barring our attempt at Westernisation by clinging to conventional customs, whether because they don't want to eat meat themselves, or because they are afraid to appear impure in the eyes of the gods. Such action is contrary to the wishes of the Emperor.'

While eating red meat is now enjoyed guilt-free, you will notice, particularly in home cooking, that red meat is not the main ingredient. There might be some meat added to vegetables and tofu to add flavour and heartiness to a stew, a stir-fry or noodles, but it is a distinctly small proportion of meat compared to the other ingredients, and compared to how much might be consumed in a similar Western dish.

In his cookbook *The Zen Kitchen*, Adam Liaw also points out that, after over a thousand years of avoiding red meat, excellent quality meat is key in Japanese cuisine: 'Japan now produces some of the best meat and poultry in the world, and yet the magnificent quality of Wagyu beef, Kurobuta pork and Cochin chickens might not have been possible without the ill-advised meat bans of the last millennium. Quality over quantity is the mantra. Meat is certainly popular in Japan these days, but the cultural hangover of centuries of presumptive taboo has meant that it is still viewed as somewhat of an indulgence.' ●

ON
INGREDIENTS

食
材
に
つ
い
て

Living outside of Japan my whole life, but constantly craving Japanese food, means I have long learned how to make these dishes with only the very basic Japanese ingredients at my disposal. It is entirely possible to cook wonderful Japanese food without many special ingredients. I know I can do most of my favourite preparations with just a handful of things: soy sauce, mirin, rice vinegar, and even powdered dashi if I cannot get katsuobushi (dried bonito flakes) and kombu (dried kelp) to make my own.

Although it is getting better where I live in Italy, it is near impossible to get most special foreign ingredients, but I am able to source the absolute essentials at the one trusty Asian grocer in the centre of Florence: soy sauce, mirin, sake, rice vinegar, katsuobushi, kombu, dried nori, two types of miso and Japanese short-grain rice.

Health-food stores often stock macrobiotic ingredients, and here I can find even more things like dried red adzuki beans for my favourite Japanese sweets, umezuke (the pickling liquid left over from pickling umeboshi, a sharp and salty condiment) and nigari (the salts used in tofu-making to coagulate soy milk). It is also here where I pick up things like tapioca starch (arrowroot) and dried mochi blocks.

At the Chinese grocer in the next town, I can find indispensable fresh produce like spring onions (scallions) and daikon, even okra and fresh corn cobs in season (an underused ingredient in Italy), as well as a lot of great pantry items, such as proper freshly made tofu, dried shiitake mushrooms (dried rather than fresh are particularly useful for

making vegetable stock – an excellent umami-rich vegetarian alternative to dashi stock), ramen noodles, soba noodles and even kinako (soybean powder for sprinkling on desserts, in cakes or on hot buttered toast).

Finally, online stores for Japanese ingredients are getting better and better, and I have happily found some wonderful sources for excellent sake and high-quality soy sauce, too. I've also supplied some recipes here in the book for making some of the ingredients that in Japan you would easily be able to pick up in a grocery store, because – well – I can't! With these you can make good, home-made versions of tonkatsu sauce, mentsuyu sauce, even panko breadcrumbs.

If I can find these things in a small town in Tuscany, where access to foreign specialty ingredients is minimal, I think that these days most of my readers will be able to find things even more easily than me, even online.

MY ESSENTIAL JAPANESE PANTRY

There is a phrase, or really an acronym, in Japanese, to help remember the unique combination of the five essential flavours so central to home cooking: *sa-shi-su-se-so* (which are also the 's' sounds of the Japanese alphabet, さしすせそ) and they stand for *sato* (sugar), *shio* (salt), *su* (vinegar), *shoyu* (soy sauce, which used to be spelled *seiu*) and miso. It's a good one if you can remember these Japanese words.

At the very minimum, the basic ingredients you need for simple Japanese cooking are the following (and I would almost put sake in there, too, because until recently I haven't been able to get it and I have been making Japanese dishes for years without, substituting mirin if necessary):

soy sauce
mirin
rice vinegar
dashi powder
miso
short-grain rice

SOY SAUCE

In Japan, you can find many different types of soy sauce (shoyu in Japanese), where often overseas there might only be one kind available. Soy sauce arrived in Japan in the 7th century from China and is made from fermented soybeans, wheat, salt and koji rice mould. Although the ingredients are more or less the same, there are various kinds of soy sauce for different uses in Japan: dark soy sauce or koikuchi, the most popular, all-purpose Japanese soy sauce, which comes from the Kanto region; light soy sauce (light in colour, but not in flavour – this is saltier) known as usukuchi; tamari, which is from central Japan and is the only completely wheat-free soy sauce; white soy sauce made with mostly wheat, which is good for dishes that you don't want to add any colour to; and finally marudaizu shoyu, a prized soy sauce made with whole beans that is especially appreciated with sashimi.

MIRIN

This rice wine is often compared to sake, but it is an entirely different ingredient. It is slightly alcoholic and quite naturally sweet and syrupy, an effect of the fermentation process. Commonly, the 'mirin' available is an imitation or 'mirin-like seasoning' and is mostly sugar with a very small, maybe 1 per cent, level of alcohol, so if you want the real thing look for 'hon mirin', which literally means 'true mirin', that has an alcohol level similar to wine. It is indispensable because it adds a complex flavour to dishes and contributes an important sweetness that balances out the ever-present salty soy sauce. When you don't have this, you can just use a bit of sugar. I've seen some recommendations suggesting to use rice vinegar as a substitute – please don't do that. Vinegar will add an acidic sharpness – the opposite of the sweetness that mirin lends – that in most cases may not be what the dish needs.

RICE VINEGAR

It is hard to find a similar vinegar to substitute for Japanese rice vinegar, which is mellower, less acidic (only 5 per cent acetic acid), sweeter and with more umami than other Western-style vinegars, like wine vinegars. It is used in making quick pickles and to flavour sushi rice, and also to balance out dressings for vegetables or in the preparation of Nanbanzuke (page 191).

DASHI POWDER

A convenient short-cut to making dashi from scratch out of katsuobushi (dried bonito flakes) and kombu (page 30), dashi powder – or even a concentrated dashi liquid that you dilute before using – may sometimes be easier to find. Dashi stock is the backbone of almost every Japanese soup and sauce, so it is handy to always have this in your pantry.

MISO

This delicious, punchy fermented soybean paste hardly needs an introduction, but like soy sauce, while many different kinds exist in Japan, overseas, you may be limited to one or two types. I like to have two kinds of miso on hand: shiro (white) miso (a younger, lighter in colour, sweeter miso) and tanshoku (brown) miso, which is a versatile, everyday miso that is made with barley or rice together with the soybeans. There is also aka (red) miso, which is deeper, darker and much stronger in flavour as it is aged. You can also mix the different miso types to customise flavours.

SHORT-GRAIN RICE

Japanese rice, a cultivar known also as Japonica rice, is unique. It is rounder, thicker, shorter and – when cooked – stickier than the more common Indica rice available throughout Asia, which is a characteristic that makes it easier to eat with chopsticks. It is often labelled as 'sushi rice' outside of Japan. There is also a glutinous rice called mochigome, which is used for making mochi like the Ohagi on page 244.

SAKE

This popular alcoholic 'wine' (a misleading term as the process is closer to beer-brewing than wine-making) made from fermenting rice is a must to accompany Japanese dishes, but you can also easily buy a 'cooking sake', which is perfectly fine to use in recipes. Sake is often added to dishes to boost umami or acidity, or even to expel strong flavours or smells in meat and fish. It is hard to substitute, but if I'm stuck, I either leave it out or add a splash of mirin in its place. Drinking sake can be such a special ritual, even just choosing the cup and vessel from which to drink. When enjoying sake with a meal, remember that during formal occasions you should not pour your own drink – someone else at the table should pour it for you, a ritual I think of as a rather lovely, convivial tradition to bring to the table – and that it can be served warmed, chilled or at room temperature.

KATSUOBUSHI

Fermented fillets of bonito or skipjack tuna are shaved into fine, feather-light flakes and are one of the two ingredients in a classic dashi stock. Katsuobushi is made by first boiling the fillets, then deboning them and removing the skin and fat. They are then wood-smoked in baskets, then sun-dried. After a few days, the now mostly dried fish is then fermented with *Aspergillus glaucus* mould culture for a couple of weeks, then sun-dried again and the mould is removed – the sun-drying, application and removal of mould cycle is repeated for months (sometimes even years) until the fillets are extremely hard and almost completely dry fillets known as honkarebushi. These can then be shaved using a special shaver on a wooden box called katsuobushi kezuriki (there is nothing quite like freshly shaved katsuobushi, my mother remembers my grandmother using one of these when she was younger). But most people use the convenient pre-shaved flakes – if you have a choice, go for thicker shavings rather than thinner, smaller ones.

KINAKO

Roasted soybean powder is a caramel-coloured, fine powder that has a naturally sweet, distinctly nutty flavour. It is quite hard to describe exactly, but it reminds me of peanut butter or sesame – if you like these flavours in sweets, you will probably like kinako. It's usually dusted on top of desserts like Anmitsu (page 238) and Warabimochi (page 250), but is delicious on ice cream and yoghurt and makes a wonderful addition to cookies and cakes (like the Kinakotokuri no keki on page 256). As it's made of whole soybeans, it is rich in vitamin B and high in protein.

KIRIMOCHI

These hard, dried mochi (rice cakes) are long-lasting and shelf-stable, so are perfect to stash in the pantry. They have a long and important history in Japan (see 'For the love of mochi', page 72). Samurai would pack these as staples to easily take and prepare on the battlefield and they are still a staple in Japanese kitchens today for making grilled snacks like Isobe mochi (page 71), celebratory New Year's soup (see Osechi Ryori for more, page 151) and in comforting sweet dishes like Zenzai (warm red bean soup, page 240).

KOMBU

Along with katsuobushi, kombu, or dried kelp, is an important umami-packed component of dashi. It is usually available in hard, dried lengths of seaweed, which may be dried flat in squares or rectangles or left wrinkled, often with a whitish mineral coating.

DRIED SEAWEED

Nori, a soft square leaf of dried seaweed, is a must for making sushi, wrapping grilled mochi or cutting into strips to top noodles, for example. Aonori are tiny flakes of green seaweed for sprinkling over okonomiyaki. Wakame is classic dried seaweed that is rehydrated and used in salad and miso soup. Hijiki is a black, stringy seaweed that is boiled before being dried, so can be simply rehydrated and then used mostly in salads and vegetable dishes.

NOODLES

Somen are very fine, thin, dried wheat-flour noodles that are often served cold in the summer. Shirataki noodles are transparent, jelly-like noodles made from konjac, or yam (so suitable for anyone who can't have wheat/gluten or eggs), usually sold packaged in liquid. Soba are thin noodles made of varying percentages of buckwheat and wheat flours and are easily found dried. They make an auspicious dish for New Year's Eve and are delicious hot or cold. Yakisoba is actually made with ramen noodles rather than true soba noodles – and ramen noodles are simply Chinese-style noodles (in fact 'ramen' comes from the Japanese pronunciation of the Chinese word for their native northern wheat flour and egg noodles: *lāmiàn*). Udon is a thick, chewy noodle made of just wheat flour and water. You can buy them dried, fresh or frozen – or easily make them by hand (page 156).

GOMA, NERI GOMA AND GOMA ABURA – SESAME SEEDS, SESAME PASTE AND SESAME OIL

Sesame has been a beloved ingredient in Japanese cuisine for thousands of years and the Japanese are still one of the world's largest consumers of this tiny seed. Sesame seeds themselves, both black and white, are used in countless ways as a condiment or garnish, or ground into gomashio or gomasio, a tasty condiment of sesame and salt used similarly to furikake. They are also ground further into a paste, neri goma, similar to tahini, which is used for dressings (like the recipe on page 129), on noodles, in dessert-making and more. Sesame oil is used for stir-frying, but also a very fragrant dressing – look for pure, unrefined Japanese sesame oil, which is a dark amber hue due to the roasting of the sesame seeds. It is delicious used in salads or as a condiment for tofu and greens.

ADZUKI BEANS

These small red beans are found dried. They are usually boiled whole with sugar or turned into a paste for a huge number of traditional sweet dishes, or cooked with rice for a celebratory auspicious dish called sekihan.

KANTEN OR AGAR AGAR

Kanten is often sold under the name 'agar agar' outside of Japan, but in reality these two seaweeds are different varieties that can be used interchangeably. Made from red algae, kanten is a plant-based gelatin used to make refreshing jellies, or even to thicken soups and preserves. The story goes that a 17th-century innkeeper discovered the properties of this seaweed after discarding a soup and finding it the next morning in jelly form. Unlike gelatin, which must be chilled to be solid, kanten jellifies at room temperature.

SHIRATAMAKO FLOUR

Perhaps one of the harder ingredients to find, this glutinous rice flour is made from mochigome or glutinous Japanese rice, which is crumbly, and in chunky granules, not a fine powder – there is also a fine glutinous Japanese rice flour called mochiko used to make certain dishes like dango. Shiratamako cannot be substituted with other types of glutinous rice flours.

KATAKURIKO – POTATO STARCH

Traditionally, katakuriko starch was made from the roots of the dogtooth violet (a plant from the lily family), but as potatoes have become more widely available and cheaper, potato starch has replaced it. It is gluten-free and used for thickening sauces, making batters fluffy and fried foods crisp. You could substitute cornflour (corn starch). When looking for Japanese katakuriko, go for one from Hokkaido, a region well known for its high-quality potatoes.

SHICHIMI TOGARASHI

This Japanese spice mix meaning 'seven spices' dates back to the 17th century and includes things like chilli, sesame seeds, nori, citrus rind, ginger and sansho or Japanese pepper. It's a popular condiment to add a subtle touch of heat to noodle dishes, rice or dishes like gyudon – think of it like adding a twist of freshly ground pepper to finish a dish.

WASABI

Sometimes called Japanese horseradish, wasabi is a must if you like a spurt of potent but short-lived heat with your sushi or sashimi or mixed into sauces. This green rhizome grows naturally in clear mountain streams and certain prefectures in Japan are famous for it, such as Shizuoka. Fresh wasabi is traditionally grated on shark-skin graters at the moment it is needed, as it loses its flavour within minutes if left uncovered – it is a world apart from some of the so-called 'wasabi' available overseas in tubes, made commonly with a mixture of Western horseradish, mustard, starch and food colouring (no actual wasabi!).

TOFU

Although this isn't exactly a pantry item, I wanted to include it among the essentials because tofu is an essential part of Japanese home cooking. Good tofu (firm or silken) can be tricky to find, often still a far cry from the fresh (as in, freshly made that same day) tofu available in Japan that is so delicious you barely need anything to even adorn it. I liken it to the difference between a proper, fresh ball of sweet, creamy buffalo mozzarella from Campania in Italy and a plastic bag of pre-shredded, rubbery 'mozzarella' that you can find in supermarkets in other countries. I have started making my own tofu at home (page 47) for the kind that you can enjoy as is. Doing this, you also get okara, the leftover soybean pulp from making tofu, which is delicious cooked with vegetables in a salad (page 130). ●

A NOTE ON OVENS

Historically, Japanese kitchens did not have ovens and, as a result, much of today's food is cooked without one; even your average Tokyo apartment won't have an oven either. In fact, the only recipes in this book that call for an oven are Western dishes adapted to Japanese tastes – cookies, cake and shokupan!

The historic word for the kitchen in Japan is kamado, or literally 'the stove', a space so symbolic that the word became synonymous with 'home' or 'family'. These stoves, which originated as open hearths in the earliest periods, became low, enclosed structures made of clay and sand, with an opening on the side for fuel and one (or two or more, depending on the household) hole on the top as the heat source – where the pots, usually earthenware or cast iron, would go.

In the Nara period, irori became very common. These were sunken pits in the centre of the room for burning charcoal, which served for heat and as a secondary stove for warming food – a hook suspended from the ceiling could hold a pot above the fire. Some well-preserved old homes still have these features.

It wasn't until the Meiji period, after Japan's isolation ended, that the change and huge influence of foreign food meant that kitchens became reorganised to suit this new-style cooking. After the Second World War, during which so many Japanese homes were destroyed, homes were rebuilt with modern, more European-style kitchens fitted out with lots of electrical gadgets. Ovens, however, were still left out. ●

COOK'S NOTES

COOKING TIMES

Recipes were tested on an induction stove top. You may need to adjust times or the heat slightly for gas or electric stove tops.

MEASUREMENTS

In these recipes, I use 20 ml (¾ fl oz) tablespoons. Cooks with 15 ml (½ fl oz) tablespoons can be generous with their tablespoon measurements. I have been mindful of this tiny difference throughout recipe testing and would like to assure you that, as this is home-style cooking, nothing will go wrong if you use 15 ml tablespoons – just taste and adjust to your liking! Cup measurements are metric, i.e. 250 ml (8½ fl oz) for 1 cup; in the US a cup is 237 ml (8 fl oz), so American cooks can be generous with their cup measurements.

OVEN TEMPERATURES

There is very little baking here for the aforementioned reasons, but where using an oven, note that if using a fan-forced or convection oven, you may need to decrease the temperature by 20°C (70°F), or adjust the baking time.

OIL FOR DEEP-FRYING

You can use any vegetable oil to fry in. I prefer seed oils, such as sunflower or rapeseed (canola) oil. Olive oil has a relatively low smoking point, so I tend to avoid it for frying and keep it for dressing. Sesame oil is a little bit trickier – personally, I keep only toasted Japanese sesame oil, which is dark in colour and aromatic and quite expensive here, so I use this for dressing, not for deep-frying, but you can also find light (same colour as regular seed oils), untoasted sesame oil, which is more neutral, and you can use this for frying and cooking with, too.

SALT

I always cook with fine sea salt. If you are using kosher salt or regular iodised table salt, you may have slightly different results, usually you'll need a little more. Please note, you do not need to salt the water for cooking noodles as you would pasta.

SUGAR

When called for, it is regular white granulated sugar. If you like, in the savoury dishes, which often call for sugar to balance the saltiness of soy sauce, you can substitute raw sugar (demerara/turbinado), which my mother often likes to do, for a slightly less sweet, nuttier flavour, or honey.

EGGS

Where possible, use free-range, organic eggs for best results. I use 55 g (2 oz) eggs, which correspond to large eggs in the US, Canada and Australia, and medium eggs in Europe. Some of the recipes call for raw eggs or yolks, which are commonly enjoyed in Japanese cuisine. If you feel unsafe doing so, simply leave them out or use pasteurised eggs, or even a cooked version (fry or poach, for example). If you are going to eat raw eggs, there are a few important things you can do to minimise further the small risk of bacteria contamination from the shell to the raw egg. First, get the freshest eggs possible and ensure there are no cracks in the shell. When cracking the egg, make sure to make a clean crack and that pieces of shell don't fall into the egg – if this happens, save that egg for a cooked dish and try again. If separating the egg, don't use the shell to separate (a popular technique), but use your hands – slightly opened fingers will strain egg white into the bowl underneath and you'll be left with a perfect yolk in your hand. Finally, use the egg as soon as possible after cracking it.

FLOUR

Flour refers to plain, all-purpose or tipo '00' flour. ●

HOME-MADE PANTRY STAPLES

'Making good dashi is the first secret of the simple art of Japanese cooking.'

—

SHIZUO TSUJI
in *Japanese Cooking: A Simple Art*

These staples are among some of the very basic pantry ingredients that I've learned how to make while living in Italy, where it is quite hard to come by Japanese ingredients. But if you live in Japan – or even Melbourne, Paris or Boston – larger urban centres where Japanese ingredients are readily available, the recipes in this chapter make ingredients that you could easily pick up in a supermarket. However, even if you can buy them, it's always nice to know that these are actually all very easy to make at home – and home-made also means you can make a simplified version that doesn't include the unwanted additives that some packaged versions of these things contain.

28

手作りの

UMAMI

うま味

One night, in 1907, Kikunae Ikeda, a professor of chemistry at Tokyo Imperial University, noticed that his soup was unusually tasty. It was the addition of kombu, which led him to study the kelp intensely to figure out how to capture this flavour. By 1909, he was not only able to isolate crystals of glutamate, simmered down from kombu stock, but he found a way to extract and package this monosodium glutamate in a seasoning that he named *ajinomoto* ('essence of flavour') and co-founded a company of the same name to produce and sell it to Japanese housewives.

He also noticed something else: 'There is a taste, which is common to asparagus, tomatoes, cheese and meat, but which is not one of the four well-known tastes.' And so Ikeda coined a new term – umami, which comes from *umai* ('delicious') and *mi* ('taste') – and proposed that this flavour, characterised by savouriness and meatiness (even if it does not derive from meat), is one of our basic tastes, along with sweetness, sourness, bitterness and saltiness.

Umami has since been detected in a number of other ingredients, the richest ones being mushrooms (especially dried shiitake), smoked or fermented fish (such as katsuobushi), shellfish, meat, green tea, Parmesan cheese and tomatoes, not to mention that first food we taste as humans: breastmilk.

Richard Hosking, in *A Dictionary of Japanese Food*, writes that umami 'is identified quite specifically with certain amino acids and nucleotides, namely monosodium glutamate (MSG), sodium inosinate and sodium guanylate. There is no question that, on the one hand, these three are important flavor enhancers and, on the other, have a powerful synergistic effect on each other, up to eight or nine times the properties of the single ingredients.'

This is one of the things that Ikeda noticed that umami flavours do – they enhance all the ingredients in a dish, making it more than the sum of its parts. Think of how Parmesan cheese, a dash of fish sauce, an anchovy, or even a squirt of ketchup, can just lift a dish. Dashi does the same in Japanese dishes. On its own, it tastes pleasant but it is very subtle. In a dish, however, like miso soup, or a noodle soup or stew, there is a deep and intense savouriness. 'All this was discovered and put into practice long before anyone knew anything about amino acids,' continues Hosking.

Why do we love umami so? Other than it makes our taste buds tingle and our mouths begin to salivate, Ikeda believed it was appealing to humans because it means proteins are present. I cannot help but think, too, of its role in breastmilk, helping encourage us as tiny humans to want more to eat. ●

29

常備食

Dashi Stock

MAKES 1 LITRE (4 CUPS)

だ
し

Dashi is probably the most important recipe to know how to make in Japanese cuisine – it is the backbone to so many dishes. It is easy to buy dashi in powder form to dissolve in hot water, or even in liquid form, also to be diluted, but be sure these only contain two ingredients, otherwise making a possibly better-quality dashi at home is so incredibly easy and it only takes minutes to make.

My obaachan would make dashi with only fish, a stock known as mizudashi. She would use niboshi (small, dried silver fish – usually baby anchovies or sardines), and would first painstakingly remove the head and entrails so there was no bitterness, then simply place the fish in a pot of water overnight to infuse. Each cook has their own way to make dashi; what usually changes is how long the katsuobushi flakes are infused for, whether or not it is brought to boiling point (some say boiling ruins the flavour of this delicate stock), and whether or not to strain or squeeze (this last about keeping the stock perfectly clear).

I think the key to a good dashi is the kombu – an umami-rich seaweed, this will lend depth of flavour. What you are doing here is heating the kombu very slowly to draw out this umami before the water gets too hot and begins to boil, which makes the kombu slimy. You want to remove the kombu before this happens. Many good cooks like to simply place the kombu in water overnight, like a cold infusion, and heat it up the next morning. If you are diligent enough to have remembered to do that, it is a great idea for extra flavour.

METHOD

Wipe the kombu with a clean cloth and place in a saucepan with 1 litre (4 cups) of cold water. Leave to steep, if you can, for at least 30 minutes (or overnight).

Set the pan over a low heat and warm until the kombu softens and the water is about to start boiling (you will see lots of tiny bubbles appear around the edges of the pan), about 10 minutes. Remove the kombu at this point – set aside if you want to make furikake with it (see opposite).

Turn the heat up ever so slightly to medium and add the katsuobushi to the kombu-infused water. Watch carefully – just as it looks as if it is about to boil, turn off the heat, skim off any scum that rises to the top of the stock, and let it steep for 5–10 minutes.

Strain the dashi through a fine-mesh sieve and it is ready to use, or store in a jar in the fridge for up to a week.

Don't throw out the precious leftover kombu and katsuobushi – they can be used to make furikake, a delicious seasoning for rice or for mixing through onigiri.

VARIATION

If vegetarian, leave out the katsuobushi and double the quantity of kombu.

30

INGREDIENTS
1 piece of kombu (dried kelp),
    about 10–15 cm (4–6 in) long
    or 10 g (¼ oz)
10 g (1 packed cup) katsuobushi
    (dried bonito flakes)

手作りの

No-Waste Furikake Rice Seasoning

MAKES 1 SMALL JAR

ふ
り
か
け

This is my favourite condiment, served on a bowl of Obaachan's rice. And now my own children's favourite way to eat rice is with a generous sprinkle of furikake on top. Instant flavour, it is also delicious sprinkled on top of eggs, salad, onigiri, or anything really.

Obaachan would keep a pot of my grandfather's favourite furikake always on hand. He would go to Tokyo's Mitsukoshi department store to buy it specially. It's called Kinshobai and, rather than the usual furikake, which is dried and has ingredients like sesame seeds, nori, dried shiso, sansho or other dried herbs, Kinshobai furikake is moist and contains pine nuts, shiitake mushrooms and katsuobushi. I have been conserving a packet in my fridge for far too long – I cannot bear to part with it, so dear it is to me as a memory of my grandparents' table. I recently came across a recipe for a home-made version of it on the website Japanese Cooking 101, and it inspired me to try my own.

Kombu and katsuobushi can be hard to find and expensive, so rather than throw them away after making dashi, this furikake is one of the best ways to reuse it. There is a Japanese expression: *mottainai* (勿体無い), which means 'regret concerning waste', and this is one of the most delicious ways to avoid mottainai, along with making tsukudani, a lovely little side dish where you slice the kombu into small pieces, then boil with water, sake, soy sauce, mirin and some sugar until the liquid is completely evaporated.

31

METHOD

Follow the directions opposite for making dashi (use it in recipes or freeze for another day). Set aside the kombu and katsuobushi. If you haven't already soaked the kombu overnight before making dashi, it is best to keep it soaking in water until you have everything ready to make the furikake.

Soak the dried mushrooms in the hot water for 15 minutes, or until they are soft enough to chop. Fish them out of the soaking liquid, remove and discard the stems, then chop the remainder into very small pieces. Filter the water they were soaking in through a fine tea strainer and place in a small saucepan.

Slice the kombu into thin strips, 1 mm (¹⁄₁₆ in) wide and 3 cm (1¼ in) long, and add to the mushroom liquid in the pan along with the mushrooms, katsuobushi and sake. Cover and simmer over a low–medium heat for about 10 minutes. Depending on how long the kombu had been soaking, it may or may not be tender enough yet, so check every now and then by taking a bite – it should be pleasantly al dente. If the liquid begins to evaporate too much and the kombu is not yet tender, top up with a bit more water. When the kombu is tender, add the mirin, soy sauce, sugar, pine nuts and sesame seeds. Continue simmering until there is practically no excess liquid left in the pan but the furikake ingredients are still moist and tender. Transfer to a bowl and let cool completely. This should keep well in an airtight container in the fridge for two weeks.

INGREDIENTS

1 piece of kombu (dried kelp), about 10–15 cm (4–6 in) long or 10 g (¼ oz)

10 g (1 packed cup) katsuobushi (dried bonito flakes) (the leftovers from making dashi, opposite, are ideal for this)

2 dried shiitake mushrooms

250 ml (1 cup) hot water

1 tablespoon sake

2 tablespoons mirin

2 tablespoons soy sauce

1 teaspoon raw sugar (demerara/turbinado)

1½ teaspoons pine nuts

1 teaspoon sesame seeds

All-Purpose Soup Base

MAKES 375 ML (1½ CUPS),
ENOUGH FOR 1.5 LITRES (6 CUPS)
OF SOUP BROTH

め
ん
つ
ゆ

32

This classic, deeply flavourful sweet-savoury sauce is a concentrated soup base for noodles like udon and soba, or for dipping tempura (you could try this with the Kakiage, page 154). If you want to make this ahead of time and have it conveniently bottled in the fridge, it keeps well for about a month.

METHOD

Place everything in a saucepan, bring to a gentle simmer and cook for 5 minutes.

Strain the sauce to remove the kombu and katsuobushi (use these in Furikake, page 31). If not using immediately, pour the mentsuyu into a jar or airtight container and keep refrigerated for up to 4 weeks.

Before serving, you should always dilute this sauce: use 1 part mentsuyu to 3 parts water (hot or cold, depending on how you plan to use it), or to suit your taste.

VARIATION

If vegetarian, simply leave out the katsuobushi, or – for extra umami – do as chef Niki Nakayama suggests: substitute the katsuobushi with dried shiitake mushrooms. I would rehydrate these in water for about an hour before starting the recipe.

INGREDIENTS

60 ml (¼ cup) sake
125 ml (½ cup) mirin
125 ml (½ cup) soy sauce
1 square of kombu, about
    5 cm (2 in) in length
    or 5 g (¼ oz)
10 g (1 packed cup) katsuobushi
    (dried bonito flakes)

手作りの

Flaky panko crumbs leave a thick, breaded coating on fried foods that is crisper and lighter than regular breadcrumbs. Indispensable for Tonkatsu (fried pork cutlet, page 218), Korokke (croquettes, page 212) or Ebi furai (fried prawn/shrimp, page 223), they are usually easily obtained in supermarkets. It's actually hard for me to find these locally, but then I discovered how easy they are to make at home – and wonderful if you have your own home-made Shokupan (Japanese milk bread, page 221), too. Crusts on or off, it's your choice (I leave them on!).

Panko Breadcrumbs

MAKES ABOUT 120 G (1½ CUPS)

パ
ン
粉

33

METHOD

If you prefer no crusts, cut them off the bread slices before using.
Blitz the bread in a food processor until torn into tiny pieces.

Spread the breadcrumbs out in a wide frying pan (skillet) and heat over a low heat, stirring constantly until the crumbs are completely dry and toasted, but not coloured, about 5 minutes. Be sure to move them all, so they don't burn.

Transfer to a tray or a wooden board in a single layer to cool down completely. Once cool, store in a jar or airtight container at room temperature and use for coating all your favourite fried dishes.

INGREDIENTS
4 slices of fresh white sandwich bread
  or Shokupan (page 221)

常備食

Tonkatsu Sauce

MAKES 625 G (2 CUPS)

と
ん
か
つ
ソ
ー
ス

Growing up, we always had a bottle of Bull-Dog Sauce in the fridge, one of Japan's oldest and most beloved tonkatsu sauces, so-named for the company mascot drawn on the front of the bottle – yes, an English bulldog, a symbol of the British inspiration behind this sauce. This 'vegetable fruit sauce' was originally developed by a shop called Misawaya in 1902. They wanted to make something similar to Worcestershire Sauce that would appeal to Japanese tastes to use on the increasingly popular Western-style dishes, such as Tonkatsu (fried pork cutlets, page 218) and other fried foods. It's a flavour that goes well with street foods, too, such as Yakisoba (page 162), Okonomiyaki (page 161) and Ebiyaki (page 165).

If you are really in a hurry and you want a very quick tonkatsu sauce made with other pantry ingredients, you could approximate a pretty good, similar flavour by mixing tomato ketchup, Worcestershire sauce, oyster sauce and some sugar or honey. But I like to go further and make a 'vegetable fruit sauce' similar to the original, which is so delicious you will want to put it on everything. Don't be put off by the long list of ingredients – it literally all just goes into a pot and is boiled together.

34

INGREDIENTS

1 small onion, thinly sliced
1 small carrot, peeled and thinly sliced
½ celery stick, thinly sliced
1 apple, peeled and thinly sliced
4–6 prunes, pitted and
    thinly sliced
2 bay leaves
1 garlic clove, sliced
3 tomatoes, such as San Marzano,
    preferably fresh, chopped
250 ml (1 cup) red wine
1 tablespoon tomato paste
    (concentrated puree)
1½ teaspoons mixed ground spices
    (cloves, coriander seed, cinnamon,
    ginger, fennel)
1 teaspoon salt
2 tablespoons water
2 tablespoons red wine vinegar
75 g (scant ½ cup) brown sugar
60 ml (¼ cup) soy sauce
80 ml (⅓ cup) Worcestershire sauce

METHOD

Place everything, except the red wine vinegar, brown sugar, soy sauce and Worcestershire sauce, in a saucepan over a medium heat and bring the mixture to a gentle simmer. Cover and cook until the vegetables and fruit are soft, about 20 minutes.

Puree the mixture (in a food processor or using a hand blender), then strain through a fine-mesh sieve until very smooth.

Return the mixture to the pan and add the red wine vinegar, sugar, soy sauce and Worcestershire sauce. Bring to a simmer over a medium heat and reduce, uncovered, for about 5 minutes, or until the sauce is thickened to your liking.

Taste for seasoning once it has cooled – you may want to add more salt or perhaps it needs a touch more sugar or a splash of vinegar. Stir through the adjustments, then pour into an airtight container (or a sterilised jar if keeping long term). This keeps very well in the fridge for several months.

手作りの

Pickled Ginger

ガ
リ

Gari are thin petals of sweet, pickled ginger, usually found alongside a plate of sashimi or sushi as palate cleansers. If you are lucky enough to grow your own ginger, or find them on offer as young rhizomes while the ginger is very fresh and still deep pink around the shoots, it is ideal for pickling. The skin should be very pale, smooth and thin, which means that you won't need to peel it at all. In Japan and most of Asia, young or 'new ginger' (新生姜) is found in the late spring, but you may want to look for it locally as its freshness and delicate skin means it doesn't travel well – in continental climates, where ginger is grown in greenhouses, the right moment for young ginger is in autumn (fall). The younger the ginger, the more likely your pickles will end up with that characteristic, naturally pinkish hue. However, if you prefer a bit more heat, older ginger (with dark beige, matte skin) is spicier.

METHOD

If using older ginger, you will first need to peel the ginger. This is easiest with a teaspoon, which might sound odd, but just try it: scrape the edge of the spoon along the skin of the ginger and it will come off very easily without wasting too much of the ginger itself. Once peeled, slice as thinly as possible; a vegetable peeler or a mandoline works well for this.

Place the ginger in a bowl and sprinkle with the salt. Massage the salt through the ginger, then leave to sit for 15–30 minutes.

Meanwhile, combine the sugar and vinegar in a small saucepan and heat until the sugar dissolves.

Rinse the salt off the ginger. If using an older ginger root (rather than a young pink one) or if you don't want this to be too spicy, blanch the ginger in boiling water for 1 minute.

Drain and squeeze the rinsed or blanched ginger out very well – I like to place it on a kitchen towel and roll it up to get the last drops of water out.

Pack into a sterilised jar or airtight container and pour over the boiling hot vinegar mixture to cover. The pickles are ready to be eaten the next day (or if you can't wait, after several hours).

These pickles last a very long time if kept refrigerated in sterilised jars. I've heard you can keep them for a year, but they don't stand a chance in our household, where pickled ginger is so loved it is stolen out of the jar as a snack at any time of the day.

INGREDIENTS

250 g (9 oz) fresh root ginger
 (the younger the better)
2 teaspoons salt
125 g (generous ½ cup) sugar
180 ml (¾ cup) rice vinegar

35

常備食

Red Pickled Ginger

MAKES ABOUT 250 G (1 CUP)

紅
生
姜

I love these little blushing ginger pickles. Punchier than gari, which is sweet and bright, beni shoga is more sour and salty, thanks to the natural properties of its pickling liquid, umesu. This is the leftover liquid from making umeboshi (pickled plums). Umeboshi are pickled when the fruit is still green and unripe, so the colour that you see umeboshi and beni shoga sporting is actually from the addition of akashiso, a purple-red-hued variety of shiso or perilla leaves. Nowadays, it is often easier to find bright red beni shoga that has been coloured with red food colouring. If you want to make this at home and forget the food colouring, it is as easy as finding a bottle of umesu (sometimes called ume plum vinegar or umeboshi vinegar) and chopping up a ginger root into matchsticks. The colour of the home-made version may come out a paler hue than you might be used to, but the flavour is fantastic. It is irreplaceable in street food dishes like Yakisoba (page 162) and Okonomiyaki (page 161) for that sour and salty kick.

36

METHOD

Peel the ginger as described on page 35, then slice into thin matchsticks, 1 mm (1/16 in) thick. Blanch the ginger in boiling water for 1 minute, then drain.

(Don't discard that ginger infusion you just made – it is wonderful at the end of a stressful day, if you have an upset stomach or if you are tired or feeling under the weather. I drink this all winter long to warm up, too. Add a spoonful of honey or a block of black sugar – see Okinawa black sugar on page 239 – and you have a soothing, calming, restoring drink.)

Spread the ginger out on a clean dish towel to dry as well as you can. Pack into a sterilised jar and cover with the vinegar. It is ready to eat the next day – if you find the flavour too overpowering, you can dilute with some water and wait another day.

These pickles last a very long time if kept refrigerated in sterilised jars.

INGREDIENTS

250 g (9 oz) fresh root ginger
250 ml (1 cup) ume plum vinegar

手作りの

常備食

JAPANESE BREAKFAST

baachan's breakfasts were the highlight of visits to my grandparents in Japan. I eagerly awaited every one of them: just-made tofu from the old lady's tofu shop across the street, firm but creamy, garnished with some freshly grated ginger and katsuobushi flakes, and a dash of soy sauce; her 'pick-me-up' pickles, in nukadoko (fermented rice bran); Natto (fermented soy beans, page 66), which admittedly I passed on, preferring the tarako (salted cod's roe grilled in its sack like a sausage) or some Niratama (egg scrambled with soy sauce and garlic chives, page 69); Miso soup (page 54) in wooden bowls, which I could smell even before coming down the stairs to the kitchen; and a bowl of the most perfect, soft, fragrant, steaming rice (page 80). Obaachan had a machine for polishing rice and she would buy brown rice and partially polish it, resulting in soft, fluffy, deliciously nutty rice that wasn't white or brown but somewhere in between. There was always a vegetable dish, perhaps spinach, squeezed tightly and cut into portions, topped again with katsuobushi and soy sauce; or – my favourite – Renkon no kinpira (lotus root and carrot slices, page 120, partially sautéed, partially braised – a great way to cook a vegetable like lotus root that is excellent at soaking up flavours).

40

朝ご

ICHIJU SANSAI: ONE SOUP, THREE DISHES

一汁三菜

The foundation of a Japanese meal is built around the concept of ichiju sansai – one soup, three dishes. From a Japanese breakfast at home to a set menu in a traditional ryokan (inn), you'll find that the classic home-cooked meal is based around this. A small bowl of soup, usually miso soup, sits to your right: Above it, there is usually a grilled dish, such as salt-grilled fish. To the left of that, a small dish, such as greens with sesame, or tofu, or perhaps even some slices of raw fish, and to the left of that a simmered dish, maybe seasonal vegetables cooked in a broth of dashi and soy sauce. A little plate of pickles and a bowl of rice are a given – they don't factor into the 'one soup, three dishes' phrase, but they are a must, no matter the occasion. The meal is complemented with green tea and finished with a piece of fresh seasonal fruit.

There is no order to how you should eat an ichiju sansai meal and that is part of the beauty of it. As Adam Liaw describes in *The Zen Kitchen*, 'Regardless of how it's served, it is always eaten by grazing across the dishes – a bite of fish here, followed by a mouthful of vegetables, a sip of soup and over to the rice, then maybe some pickles to cleanse the palate before heading back for another sip of soup.' ●

41

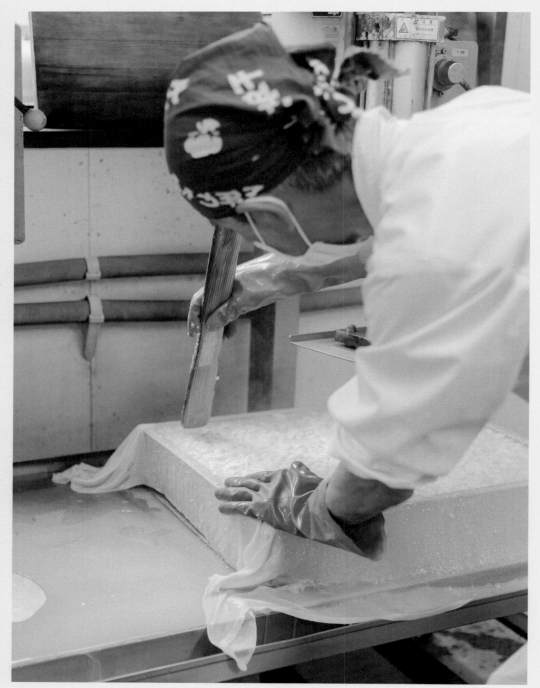

Tofu making in Nagano at Sennen Tofu.

朝ご

MAKING TOFU
IN THE MOUNTAINS OF NAGANO

長
野
の
山
麓
で
の
豆
腐
づ
く
り

My grandparents, living in an area with many Buddhist temples, were spoiled for choice when it came to fresh tofu shops on their street. I remember those old-fashioned shops, fast-disappearing now: a room with a spartan, concrete floor and stainless steel vats of water holding the morning's just-made tofu, with a smiling old woman selling them.

I travel to Chino, a two-hour train ride from Tokyo, to the foothills of Nagano's mountain ranges, to learn how to make fresh tofu with Kobayashi-san, who makes tofu for all the local schools and sells the rest through his tiny store, Sennen Tofu. He is about to turn seventy, but you wouldn't guess it from his spritely energy as he runs from one part of his laboratory to another, gathering the equipment to show me how to make a batch of tofu. It's only 10 a.m., but his day began at 3 a.m. to make tofu for the schools. He starts with soybeans – these have been soaked for 20 hours and they are plump and shiny, piled high in the top of a contraption – rather like a giant pressure cooker – that both purees and cooks them in mere minutes. Fresh spring water from the mountains is added to the soybeans as they get sucked into the machine. I ask him whether the

mountain water is something that makes this tofu special and he nods – it is full of natural minerals. But also, Kobayashi-san points out, the weather, season and altitude affect the whole process, too. The way he makes tofu is particular to this area.

Next, the bean pulp is separated from the liquid: fresh, boiling hot soy milk pours into a large bucket and okara, the dry, crumbly soybean pulp, into another. The okara is a delicious side product and used for stirring through salads and side dishes – it is excellent at soaking up good flavours. He adds a saucepanful of cool spring water to the soy milk to cool it down. 'The most important thing about making tofu is the temperature of the soy milk when you put the nigari in,' he tells me. Nigari, also known as bittern, is the leftover salts from evaporating salt water. My mind is racing, wondering how the first person discovered that these salts – mostly magnesium, calcium and potassium – could coagulate soy milk and turn it into tofu. 'Too hot and it becomes very hard; too cool and it won't set.' The ideal temperature is somewhere between 75 and 80°C (167 and 176°F). It seems such a modern, chemistry-driven process that it amazes me how unchanged tofu-making is from its ancient methods – quite like cheesemaking.

Kobayashi-san checks the temperature again. He prepares his nigari solution, dissolving the salts in some water in a jug. It is a tiny amount compared to the huge bucket of steaming soy milk. He pours it in, then very gently and very briefly swirls a stick – called a kai – through the bucket to distribute the nigari. 'It's like a sensor,' says Kobayashi-san, since you can feel through the kai how dense the tofu is becoming. Now we wait a moment. I can already see the soy milk begin to separate and form lumps. Having made cheese many times, I can't help but see the parallels, and it just becomes more and more similar. As we wait, chunky, soft clouds of curd float towards the surface. 'Oboro,' Kobayashi-san explains, 'Like baby tofu.' He scoops some out into dishes and hands me one. It's so creamy, like the very best, wobbly, melt-in-the-mouth crème caramel, and it takes me right back to central Sicily,

43

where just a few weeks earlier I had tasted the first fresh curds of a pecorino just as the shepherd had swirled rennet through the hot sheep's milk.

He mixes the soy milk again, but gently, so as not to break up the other 'baby tofus' underneath, which helps give a soft, fluffy texture to the final tofu. He is also looking for the soy milk to change colour from creamy opaque to slightly transparent – this is called yu, and it looks exactly like curds and whey. He scoops the mixture out, pouring the curds into a prepared 'bed' for the tofu, a tray with holes covered with a fine cheesecloth (muslin), which is then pressed, first by Kobayashi-san himself and then with the machine, where a plank of wood is pushed down over the top of the bed of curds, squeezing out the excess yu. Moments later, the tofu is turned out onto a floating board in a huge vat of fresh spring water and sliced. In a matter of half an hour the first batch of tofu is done.

We sat down to taste it – my favourite part. First, I was told, I must taste it on its own, then the next bite should be with a pinch of salt and some egoma (perilla seed) oil, which the locals grow themselves in community fields with laborious harvests. It is a highly prized, fragrant oil, a little similar to sesame oil but more herby than nutty, that has been long appreciated in East Asian countries for its medicinal properties as much as for its use in the kitchen. It might be my favourite new flavour discovery. Finally, we try it with soy sauce – and that bite tasted like my obaachan's breakfast. ●

44

45

大絹豆腐　厚揚　豆乳　おから

はん

JAPANESE BREAKFAST

朝ご

My favourite way with tofu is hiyayyako (chilled tofu), which is to be enjoyed when you have good, freshly made tofu that is so delicious that you barely need to add anything to it. It is admittedly harder to find this kind of tofu outside of Asia, but making tofu at home is not only do-able but fun – and it is a game-changer. If you would like to give it a try, follow this recipe; otherwise, if you already have access to a nice block of fresh tofu, see the Hiyayyako recipe on page 50 for ideas on how to dress it. By making your own fresh tofu, you will also have a huge batch of okara (soybean pulp) left over, which you can use in the Okara salad recipe on page 130.

You will need some specific tools to make tofu: a sugar thermometer, cheesecloth (muslin), and a wooden tofu mould (about 18 cm × 18 cm/7 in × 7 in) that has removable sides and holes in the bottom – or a makeshift equivalent (a strainer or even a cheese mould could do the job, although you may have a round tofu instead of a square block). If you have a precision scale, that's great, as measuring the nigari salt can be tricky even with a regular digital scale (the teaspoon measurement given below is approximate but because the form of nigari can be irregular it isn't very precise). If you add too much you will have a firmer tofu. Nigari can be found in health-food or specialty stores.

Fresh Home-made Tofu

MAKES 6 SERVINGS
(ABOUT 500 G/1 LB 2 OZ)

手作りのとうふ

47

METHOD

Before starting, make sure you have a clean kitchen and sink. Unless you have kitchen helpers, it helps too to have all the ingredients measured out and the equipment set up. In preparation, have ready a fine-mesh sieve, a large, heavy-based saucepan or cast-iron or earthenware pot, a spatula or wooden spoon, and your tofu mould (or a strainer set over a bowl), which should be prepared with a damp cheesecloth laid carefully over it.

Rinse the soybeans and place in a large bowl of water to soak for a day. Top up with water whenever you notice there is not enough to cover them.

The next day, drain the soybeans and place in a food processor or blender along with the measured spring water. Blend until very creamy – you may need to do this in two batches. Pour the puree into a large, heavy-based saucepan and set over a medium heat. You will need to stir slowly as it heats to a simmer, to ensure nothing gets stuck or burns on the bottom of the pan. Skim off the froth on the top of the puree. Continue cooking and stirring until you have a consistency like a runny polenta, about 15 minutes.

Now you need to separate the soy milk from the pulp with a cheesecloth-lined strainer or a fine-mesh sieve set over a pot. You can use the same one as before, as long as it is completely clean. (The important thing here is that the soy milk goes into a vessel that is good at keeping the temperature stable, so a cast-iron or earthenware pot with a lid, that holds the heat better *Cont. >*

INGREDIENTS

400 g (generous 2 cups)
  dried yellow soybeans
2 litres (8 cups) spring or mineral water
  (if possible – mineral water will give
  the smoothest result)
3 g (about 1 teaspoon) nigari salt,
  or 1½ tablespoons liquid nigari

はん

A heavy-based pan that is good at holding heat is best for tofu-making, particularly during the time when you've placed the nigari in the warm soy milk and you are waiting for the curds. It really needs to stay at a constant temperature, so be mindful of this, as well as the climate and temperature of the room. If it is cold, for example, the temperature can drop in the pan too and the oboro may not form well. But tofu-making is forgiving – you can simply heat the pan again if this has happened. You can even add a bit more nigari if you suspect that you didn't add enough the first time. Just keep in mind that too much heat or too much nigari will result in firmer, harder tofu, which you should try to find a balance for – ideally this home-made tofu should be a slightly firm tofu but with a soft, fluffy texture.

than a metal or plastic bowl, is ideal. If it gets too cold too quickly, the tofu won't form properly and you will need to heat it up again, so it's much easier to just start in a good pot – that way if you can see the temperature is falling, you can always turn on the heat slightly to keep it warm.) Push as much liquid as you can from the mixture (the leftover okara can be saved to use in a salad, page 130).

Check the temperature of the soy milk, it should be between 75 and 80°C (167 and 176°F); if it is cooler than this, heat it back up gently. If it is too cool, it won't set, and if it is too hot, it will be too hard, so checking with a thermometer is best.

Meanwhile, prepare the nigari solution. Often, nigari comes as a clumpy, wet salt, or you may also be able to find it in liquid form. As a salt, it should be dissolved in some water. It isn't so important how much water you add – the salt doesn't interact with the water, only with the soy milk, and the water will be pressed out of the tofu later. But for this amount, about 2 tablespoons of water should be enough.

When the soy milk has come to the right temperature, remove from the heat, add the nigari and slowly but briefly stir it through. Cover and let the soy milk sit for 3–5 minutes, then slowly, briefly stir with a spatula to the bottom of the pan. You should now see the oboro (curds) – be careful not to break these little clouds up or you will have a tougher tofu. Cover and let sit for a further 3–5 minutes, making sure to keep the pot warm, ideally at a constant temperature (see note). What you are looking for after the second rest is for plenty of fluffy oboro and the yu (the liquid around it) should now be turning transparent rather than opaque. If not, it may just need a bit more time; give it another gentle stir, then put the lid back on, keep warm and wait a further 10 minutes.

Once you see the yu is transparent and you have plenty of thick, creamy clumps of oboro, you can carefully scoop out the oboro with a slotted spoon into the cheesecloth-lined tofu mould. Fold the cheesecloth carefully and neatly back over the top of the tofu so it is fully enclosed, then with the wooden top of the frame (or an equivalent if using a makeshift mould – a plate, for example), press firmly and hold for a minute or so to remove most of the excess liquid. You can keep pressing with your own weight for several more minutes or you can simply place a weight on the top of the tofu – 2 tins of tomatoes, for example, would be ideal – and leave for about 5–10 minutes. The harder and longer you press, the firmer the tofu, so adjust as you wish.

Remove the frame and place the whole block of tofu in a deep container filled with cool water and unwrap the cheesecloth gently. You can now slice the tofu (still submerged) into serving-portion blocks, or if you used a sieve and have an odd-shaped piece, you can cut it into smaller cubes. Use a sharp knife and a slicing motion rather than pushing down onto the tofu for the best cut. Enjoy it immediately or store the tofu in this water in an airtight container in the fridge for 3–5 days. Tofu also freezes well.

はん

Chilled Dressed Tofu

SERVES 1

冷
奴

Personally, my favourite dressing for cold tofu is how my obaachan would prepare it (with spring onions/scallions, ginger and katsuobushi with soy sauce), but there are countless ways you can enjoy this dish – these are my top five. If I ever get my hands on some fresh shiso leaves or fresh myoga (Japanese ginger shoots – incredibly fragrant, crisp shoots, served finely chopped), I find them irresistible paired with fresh tofu. Sweet cherry tomatoes go well, too, and in that case I would pair with chives and either sesame oil or ponzu sauce.

INGREDIENTS

per 120 g (4½ oz) serving of fresh, chilled tofu

VERSION 1
a thumb-sized piece of fresh root ginger, peeled and finely grated
1 spring onion (scallion), both white and green parts, finely chopped
1 heaped tablespoon katsuobushi (dried bonito flakes)
1 teaspoon soy sauce

OPTIONAL
1 fresh shiso leaf, 1 teaspoon sesame oil (or egoma/perilla seed oil)

VERSION 2
4–5 chives, finely chopped
3–4 cherry tomatoes, quartered and marinated for 10 minutes with a pinch of salt
1 teaspoon ponzu sauce

VERSION 3
thinly sliced cucumber (as prepared in the cucumber salad on page 119)

VERSION 4
okra (as prepared on page 126)

VERSION 5
1 tablespoon Natto (page 66)
1 spring onion (scallion), both white and green parts, finely chopped
1 small square of nori seaweed, finely cut into strips

OPTIONAL
sprinkling of toasted sesame seeds or shichimi togarashi

METHOD

To prepare, pat your serving of tofu dry with a clean dish towel and place on a small dish. Pile the chosen ingredients on top of the tofu, then add the sauce or oil over the top, if using.

50

朝ご

はん

My Mother's Lemon-Pickled Daikon

MAKES 1 × 250 ML (8½ FL OZ) JAR

大
根
の
浅
漬
け

I messaged my mother, Sumie, one day to ask her how she does her pickled daikon, which is, for me, one of the most Japanese flavours ever. I love dipping into a little side of these pickles at breakfast or really with any meal. She sent back a one-sentence explanation: 'After sprinkling salt over slices of daikon, drain water and marinate with vinegar, lemon slices and a bit of sugar if I feel like it!' I was getting used to figuring out these kinds of instructions on my own, but I wrote back: 'Lemon slices only or juice too?' 'I like both. Try adjusting how you like it,' she wrote back, shortly followed by, 'I add lemon in everything.'

And that is precisely how Japanese pickles should be approached – *try adjusting how you like it*. Keep in mind that lemons can vary greatly in acidity – my mother has Meyer lemons, so these are on the sweeter side. If using other kinds of lemons, you may need to adjust the sugar to balance out the acidity. I personally like just the lemon slices in here and this is how the recipe is written below, but if you want to add lemon juice to the pickling liquid too, do so as you combine the rice vinegar and sugar – again, you may need to taste and adjust the sugar to keep the balance.

These are so easy to make because they are a form of 'quick pickling' – you can enjoy them after only a couple of hours – and you can always adjust the sweetness, sourness or even spiciness (with the addition of ginger or chilli, for example) to your liking. But if you ask me, these are the best pickles. It's the slices of lemon that do it for me.

52

METHOD

Peel and slice the daikon into 2–3 mm (⅛ in) slices and then cut the slices into halves or quarters, depending on how large the daikon circumference is. Place them in a bowl and sprinkle over the salt, rubbing it through so that it is well distributed. Leave for 5–10 minutes. This will help draw out extra moisture. Rinse and pat dry really well with a clean dish towel.

Combine the rice vinegar and sugar in a jar and shake or stir the mixture until the sugar is dissolved. Add the daikon and lemon pieces to the jar and let marinate for a couple of hours before eating.

Keep leftovers in their jar in the fridge; these last really well, if you don't eat them all at once.

INGREDIENTS

1 × 10 cm (4 in) piece of daikon
  (about 150 g/5½ oz)
¼ teaspoon salt
125 ml (½ cup) rice vinegar
1½ tablespoons sugar, or to taste
½ lemon, cut into thin slices,
  then quarters

朝ご

はん

Miso Soup

MAKES 4 SMALL JAPANESE-STYLE
MISO BOWLS

味
噌
汁

54

This beloved soup is part of every breakfast. The variations are endless, so you may never have the same soup twice. I think this may have been the first Japanese dish that my mother taught me how to make (such a simple and quick recipe for young people to learn how to prepare) and I will always remember her advice: the key to a good miso soup is to never let the miso boil, it flattens the flavour of the soup.

Potato and onion are a classic combination for miso soup and easy ingredients to find anywhere, but I also love kabocha pumpkin (leave the skin on) in place of the potato, or the addition of wakame seaweed. See the variations below for more ideas and use this very easy formula: place root vegetables (daikon, carrot, potato) first in the cold dashi and cook until soft, usually not more than 10 minutes. Next, add any quick-cooking vegetables (such as mushrooms or spinach) for the last minute or two, and delicate ingredients (tofu, seaweed, clams) right at the end just to warm through – do not overcook these. Stir through the miso off the heat; if adding spring onion (scallion), sprinkle over the top at the end.

METHOD

Peel and slice the potato into bite-sized pieces. I usually cut it into 2–3mm (⅛ in) slices and then cut these into quarters. Thin, small pieces will cook fairly quickly. Place these in a bowl of cold water for a few minutes to rinse off the extra starch, then drain them and add to the dashi.

Place the cold dashi in a saucepan, add the potato pieces and bring to a simmer over a medium heat. Cook for about 5 minutes, then add the onion and continue cooking until the vegetables are tender but not falling apart, a further 3–5 minutes should do it, depending on the vegetables. Turn off the heat and stir in the miso paste. (As miso paste is so thick, it is usually first stirred with some of the dashi to help loosen it in a special kind of strainer, similar to a tea strainer but deeper. You can use a ladle too, but the strainer actually works very nicely to capture the barley residue inside brown miso, for a completely smooth miso. If you don't have one of these, it's not a problem if the residue ends up in the soup – you can still eat it and actually I quite like finding the little grains at the bottom of my miso bowl.) Taste – if it is too strong for your liking, dilute with a little more dashi or water, or add a tiny bit more miso if you find it too shy, then serve immediately.

VARIATIONS

Try some of these combinations instead: diced tofu and wakame seaweed; daikon batons and sliced aburaage (twice-fried tofu); clams and spring onions (scallions); diced tofu and mushrooms like shimeji or shiitake; pumpkin (winter squash) and onion; Chinese (napa) cabbage or carrot; sliced long eggplant (aubergine), boiled in the dashi until silky soft, pairs nicely with aburaage or gobo (burdock root) cut into matchsticks, or spring onions; a favourite of mine is clams (page 56).

INGREDIENTS

1 small potato (about 50 g/1¾ oz)
500 ml (2 cups) Dashi
  (page 30), cold
½ small onion, thinly sliced
3–4 tablespoons brown miso paste

朝ご

はん

Clear Soup with Clams

SERVES 4 AS PART OF A JAPANESE
BREAKFAST OR BIGGER MEAL

あ
さ
り
の
吸
い
物

Next to the Kinpira dish of braised lotus root and carrot (page 120), my obaachan's Asari no suimono is one of the reasons I looked forward to each visit to Japan. For me, it is an incredible dish because of its very few ingredients and the fact that it takes just minutes to make. It really relies on the flavour of the freshest live clams, which are the star, but also the careful drawing out of all the umami flavour from the kombu. Also important is sake, which is used sparsely but adds incomparable flavour to the dish – without it the dish tastes incomplete. It is an excellent example of how incredibly simple Japanese home cooking is, and how attention to the preparation of each quality ingredient brings out the flavour to make a harmonious, nourishing, memorable dish.

Note that the servings here are for Japanese-style miso bowls, which are small.

56

INGREDIENTS

250 g (9 oz) live clams, such as
   vongole veraci, rinsed and purged
   (see opposite)
1 piece of kombu, about 5 cm (2 in)
   square, or 5 g (¼ oz)
500 ml (2 cups) cold water
½ teaspoon salt
1 tablespoon sake

METHOD

Place everything in a saucepan over the lowest heat and slowly bring to a gentle simmer. This slow heating is key to drawing out the flavour from the kombu. Just before the water begins to boil, remove the kombu, otherwise it will become bitter and slimy (reserve it and you can use it to make home-made Furikake, page 31). Continue cooking until the clam shells have just opened, 1–2 minutes. Serve immediately.

VARIATION

You can turn this into a miso and clam soup by stirring in some white or brown miso right at the end – use 1 tablespoon of miso per person.

朝ご

Ensure that the clams have been purged before starting this dish. If you've bought your clams in a supermarket or they are vacuum-packed, they are likely to be ready to go (you can always ask your fishmonger for confirmation), but do always rinse them before using. If you need to purge them, follow these steps:

1. Place the clams in a large glass or ceramic bowl or shallow dish that can ideally hold the clams in one layer, allowing them to open more easily.

2. Cover the clams in salt water (use 2 tablespoons of sea salt for every 1 litre/4 cups of water) to a depth of 2–3 cm (about 1 in). To avoid shocking them to death, try not to put them in water that is dramatically different from the temperature they have been kept in.

3. Leave the clams to purge for about 1 hour, but not too much longer. If you need to leave them longer, make sure you change or add more salt water to keep them from dying.

4. When ready to use, remove the clams with a slotted spoon or with your hands to a colander rather than tip the water out directly into the colander – you will just end up pouring any purged sand back over the top of them.

朝ご

My favourite part of a traditional Japanese breakfast is the fish – often served whole with blistered skin, with only salt as the one other ingredient to capture the flavour and improve the texture – the salt helps firm up the fish. It is usually served with a little garnish of grated fresh daikon or a wedge of lemon, or both. Whole aji (Japanese horse mackerel), or amberjack, also known as hamachi (yellowtail) are often used. I find these harder to get where I live, but I also adore whole saba (mackerel) cooked this way or wild-caught salmon fillets. We usually buy whole mackerel, which is beautiful in season in the autumn (fall) and winter, and fillet it at home, but otherwise ask your fishmonger to do this for you.

Grilled Fish

SERVES 4 AS PART OF
A JAPANESE BREAKFAST

INGREDIENTS

4 × 2.5 cm (1 in) thick slices of wild-caught salmon (about 200 g/7 oz) or 4 mackerel fillets, skin on
¾ teaspoon salt
a splash of sake, if you have it
vegetable oil, for greasing
lemon wedges or grated daikon, to serve

NOTE

I look for wild-caught salmon, I do not buy farmed salmon. It costs more, but is a treat so we eat it less. To differentiate from wild salmon (where the fish is entirely born and raised naturally in a native area – for example Pacific salmon in Alaska), wild-caught salmon is fish caught in its natural habitat. Usually, these salmon begin in hatcheries, where the young fish are marked (such as a clip on the fin) and then released into the wild. Any salmon that has had part of its life manipulated by humans is called 'wild-caught'. They still eat a natural diet, do things wild salmon do and live in their native environment, and they are also genetically and nutritionally similar to wild salmon, but, importantly, they don't cut into dwindling native populations. For this reason, wild-caught salmon are considered the more sustainable of salmon options at the moment. They are much better for the planet than farmed salmon as they live their lives like wild salmon – no pesticides, hormones or pollutants. Arctic char and trout are similar fish that are wonderful grilled this way, as are mackerel and sardines. Check msc.org, mcsuk.org and goodfish.org.au for more information on sustainable seafood near you.

59

METHOD

Rinse and pat the fish dry. With a sharp knife, lightly score the skin side of the fillets several times on the diagonal. Season the fillets with a generous pinch of salt on all sides, then sprinkle over some sake if you have it too – this is to take away any fishy smell. Place them on a baking tray lined with kitchen paper and let sit for 30 minutes in the fridge. When ready to cook, rinse the fish of any excess salt, then pat the fish dry very well.

Heat a heavy-based frying pan (skillet) over a medium–high heat. If using mackerel fillets, I like to cover the pan with a round of baking paper so the skin does not stick to the pan; it will still brown and crisp beautifully. Add a dash of vegetable oil to grease the pan (or the baking paper, if using) and wipe away any excess with kitchen paper, particularly if using salmon, as it is quite oily already. Place the fish skin-side down in the pan and cook for 3½–5 minutes, uncovered, or until you can see the flesh become opaque and turn from pink to brown. The skin should be browned and totally crisp. If using salmon, turn it over and continue cooking until just cooked (note that for wild salmon the cooking time is quicker than for farmed salmon, which tends to be plumper; 5–6 minutes in total will be fine for wild salmon, about 10 minutes for the latter). If using mackerel, you do not need to turn the fish, just cook it on one side – you will avoid overcooking it this way. The skin should be crisp and the flesh juicy.

Serve the fish skin-side up with a wedge of lemon or some grated daikon (squeeze out any excess liquid) on the side.

朝ご

This classic Japanese egg omelette is something I have loved since I was a child. It's the perfect balance between sweet and savoury. When I find it in a bento box or a platter of nigiri sushi, it is the one I will save for the last bite, as it is my favourite, but it is also delicious just served on its own as part of a breakfast. It is a must for Futomaki sushi rolls (page 89) or hand-rolled Temaki sushi (page 97). My mother always said that you could tell a good sushi place not by the fish but by how good the tamagoyaki is, so when I discovered at Tsukiji market – Tokyo's famous fish market – that there is a stall dedicated just to tamagoyaki, which is sold on a stick to a constant queue of people, I knew I had found my favourite snack.

I will admit, it takes a fair bit of practice to get the roll just right. You also need to know your pan well and keep it at the right temperature, as it is crucial not to let the egg brown too much to keep the omelette sweet and creamy. In Japan, a special rectangular pan called makiyakinabe is used to form these into a nice shape, but you can make them in a round pan as well, the technique is the same. These pans are usually made of lined copper or cast iron, as both hold heat well and evenly and are non-stick – very important whenever frying eggs. The pan I use is 15 cm × 18 cm (6 in × 7 in) and rectangular.

To learn how to perfect these, I asked for some help from my friend Yuta Mizoguchi, who is a brilliant sous chef at one of my favourite restaurants, Maggese, in San Miniato. Before moving to Tuscany, he worked in a ryokan in his native Japan and tamagoyaki is one of his specialties. 'It's very important to have everything ready and be organised,' he tells me. As a chef used to working in a small space, I noticed his set-up included a small bowl of oil with a piece of kitchen paper folded a few times over. The oil is used to grease the pan thoroughly and pretty generously in between each flip; I had noticed this being done in Tsukiji market, too, where the chef uses saibashi, long chopsticks, to pick up the oil-soaked kitchen paper to quickly grease all parts of the pan. He also has the beaten egg mixture ready with a small ladle and a bamboo mat, the kind you use for rolling sushi, ready and waiting to place the tamagoyaki in when it is cooked to help give it a nice, rectangular shape.

Cont. >

Rolled Egg Omelette

MAKES 1 ROLL (6 PIECES)

卵
焼
き

61

はん

METHOD

Choose a small pan that conducts heat well and evenly (ideally one that you already know is good for cooking eggs in; a non-stick or cast-iron pan is a good choice, for example). Prepare a small bowl with a couple of tablespoons of oil and some absorbent kitchen paper folded a few times over to grease in between layers of omelette. Grease the pan lightly with the oil.

In a bowl, beat the eggs together with the remaining ingredients.

Heat the pan over a medium heat. Using a small ladle, pour in about a quarter of the egg mixture and tip the pan so that it forms a thin layer, almost like a crepe. Let it bubble away, poking the bubbles as they appear with chopsticks, and letting the holes fill with more egg. Cook until it just begins to set but is still custardy and not yet browning. Roll up the omelette away from you, then use chopsticks or tongs to pick up the absorbent paper, dip it in the bowl of oil and quickly oil the exposed part of the pan. Push the entire omelette roll back towards you in the pan and finish oiling the rest of the pan. Now pour another ladle of egg mixture into the exposed part of the pan. Cook as before, then roll the egg roll over the new layer, away from you. Grease the exposed part of the pan, as before, push the egg roll back towards you, and grease the rest of the pan. Keep going in this way until you have used up the whole egg mixture.

When finished, tip the egg roll onto a bamboo mat and roll it up, using the mat to give it a nice, uniform shape – this is an especially good step if you didn't use a square pan. Keep it held there for a couple of minutes until cooled slightly. Now you can cut the roll into thick slices and enjoy warm, or wait until fully cooled and add to bento boxes, or slice into long strips lengthways for temaki or futomaki.

62

INGREDIENTS

vegetable oil, for greasing
3 eggs
½ teaspoon soy sauce
1 teaspoon raw sugar
   (demerara/turbinado)
1 tablespoon Dashi (page 30) or water

朝ご

NATTO:
THE DIVISIVE
FERMENTED SUPERFOOD

納
豆

64

This dish of slimy, nutty, fermented soybeans – natto – divides my family. My obaachan, mother and sister, in particular, adore natto and could eat it every day for breakfast, but my grandfather called them 'rotten beans' and couldn't understand why anyone would want to eat them. My mother believed it was because he was from Kyushu – she has a theory that people from southern Japan don't enjoy natto as they didn't grow up with it. In the north, it's not unusual for natto to be fed to babies so that they develop an appreciation for it early in life. In fact, the regional preference makes sense. Compared to Tokyo and the rest of the Kanto region in the eastern part of the country and northern Japan, where rice is the main staple, in southern Japan, rice competes with a great tradition of noodles and other starchy dishes like Okonomiyaki (page 161) – and natto is arguably best eaten on top of warm, fluffy rice, which makes it easier to pick up with chopsticks and is also a foil to the unusual texture of the beans.

Natto is made by first soaking whole yellow soybeans at room temperature for 20 hours. They are then steamed for about 40 minutes. After cooling to 40–50°C (104–122°F), they are infused with a pure culture of *Bacillus subtilis natto* and kept for 24 hours at 40°C (104°F) in shallow trays made of wood or polystyrene (but once upon a time, the trays were made of rice straw, which contained the original starter for natto fermentation in the form of naturally occurring bacteria). The beans are then aged at a cool temperature for up to a week. During the fermentation process, long chains of polyglutamic acid form, covering the beans with a white coating and creating the characteristic stringy slime, a texture the Japanese call *neba neba*, which is what is so appreciated by those who love natto. This acid is also responsible for giving natto its unique, deeply umami flavour.

The historical process of making natto possibly arrived in the early Yayoi period, along with rice and soybeans, when there was an exchange of cultural traditions from Korea and China to Japan. But there are plenty of old local legends, too, such as the one of the celebrated 11th-century samurai and shogun (commander in chief) Minamoto no Yoshiie, whose troops were attacked while they were boiling soybeans. They hastily packed up the beans in straw bags, mounted their horses and left, not opening the beans for a few days. When they finally opened them and discovered the beans had fermented, they tasted them and discovered they were good – and even approved by the shogun. It is said that the word *natto* (納豆) comes from the Japanese phrase of 'beans for the shogun' (将軍 に 納めた 豆, *shogun ni osameta mame*), referring to a practice where beans were sometimes used as a form of payment.

Like many fermented foods, natto is gaining some attention internationally for its superfood status: positive gut and probiotic benefits and antibacterial powers that studies have shown help prevent everything from strokes (its special 'nattokinase' enzyme helps thin blood) to osteoporosis to depression. But in Japan it's not just a superfood – it is a beloved everyday breakfast; a very economical (100 yen for three–four servings) and highly nutritious dish that goes perfectly with rice and needs almost no preparation – easy to buy and easy to eat.

However, there is one drawback. To someone who hasn't grown up with natto, it is undoubtedly the consistency of the sticky mucus covering the beans that immediately polarises people, too closely reminiscent of bodily fluids that provoke disgust. You either love it or you hate it. For those who love it, it is precisely this slimy texture that is appreciated, and in fact, in Japan you can find a number of important ingredients that have it and are enjoyed for the slime factor. Okra, for example, is boiled until the mucilaginous consistency is at its best, and yamaimo, mountain yam, is grated to get the maximum effect. Nameko mushrooms and several types of seaweed, such as mozuku and mekabu, are equally slimy. These ingredients not only play an important role in simple vegetable dishes, but they are often combined with natto itself for a sort of double-slime effect!

Almost always served chilled, accompanying or on top of a bowl of hot rice, the usual way to enjoy natto is first to squeeze over a tiny packet of hot, bright yellow Japanese karashi mustard (similar to hot English mustard) and a few drops of soy sauce. You then must whisk the beans with your chopsticks until the sticky mucilage becomes pale and creamy – some only mix it in, but enthusiasts have been known to whip them one hundred, two hundred, even up to four hundred times, until very airy, as you might egg whites. There are even special chopsticks that you can buy that are specifically for whipping natto. It not only brings out the nutty, umami flavour, but the whipping also intensifies the slimy consistency – though some might prefer to describe it as silky.

The flavour of natto is not what is particularly strong, but rather its smell. I personally find it rather appealing, reminiscent of other fermented things I love, such as the smell of opening a packet of fresh yeast, and Parmesan rind. Even something

of Australian Vegemite. But as a child (even though I was an adventurous eater, willing to try anything), seeing the long, sticky, fine strands of slime attached to my mother's chopsticks, along with my grandfather's lamentations, was enough to put me off even trying it and, as a result, I avoided it for nearly forty years.

When I began asking my natto-loving family members for their favourite ways to eat it, I noticed a certain excitement when people describe how they eat natto. This is not a dish you get a shrug and an average response about – eyes light up, a smile begins to curl at the corner of a mouth and they jump into recounting the 'best' way to enjoy natto on rice. The enthusiasm is contagious.

My mother is a traditionalist and enjoys natto with the hot Japanese mustard and soy sauce that it usually comes with, but sometimes she will add some ground sesame seeds or cucumber, which add a contrasting and welcome crunch. My sister Hana likes it this way but with pieces of chopped avocado added as well. My cousin Yoshie tops her natto with medamayaki – a fried egg, sunny-side up, with a splash of soy sauce – and her children have inherited her love for this breakfast, too. My uncle Daisuke prefers his with finely sliced spring onions (scallions) and a very fresh, raw egg yolk mixed through, which intensifies the gooey nature of the natto. My aunt Hideko, who has Korean roots, likes it with kimchi, but she tells me if that is hard to find I should try it with spaghetti, too. Toshio, another cousin, makes it in a mouthwatering way: first, he quickly stir-fries some minced (ground) pork with sesame oil, garlic and garlic chives. Once it has cooled down a bit, he stirs through the natto with its mustard and soy sauce. I can see how, in a dish like this, you need the rice to help soak up all the flavours from the bottom of the pan.

It is also popular with dried seaweed, cheese or a touch of chilli oil. And although rice is the default, I found there were even more ways you could make a satisfying natto breakfast – add it to miso soup (this reduces its slimy texture), pop it in a grilled cheese sandwich or even in an omelette. ●

Yoshie's Natto

SERVES 1

納
豆

My cousin Yoshie, who is a great cook like her mother Hideko and our obaachan, usually serves natto to her children with a fried egg on top. But she also makes these versions below with raw egg, which I feel is pure home cooking, the ultimate nostalgic dish of a Tokyo childhood. Similar to a raw egg tamago no gohan, this is one for people who appreciate the creaminess of raw egg yolk, silky natto and cloud-like rice. Although I am forty years late to the natto party, somehow, many years after my grandparents' passing, I find myself hanging on to any memory of them that I can. And the one of an everyday, ordinary breakfast and the nutty smell of natto in Obaachan's kitchen is just the kind of memory I'm trying to preserve.

66

METHOD

Whip the natto really well. Usually it comes with some soy sauce and mustard, and you can choose to add these to season the natto, along with the dashi powder to give it a little extra flavour, but what is important is vigorously whipping the natto with chopsticks (or a fork) until it becomes very silky and creamy – whip like you would egg whites to make them frothy. Place this on top of the warm rice and enjoy plain or top with one of the following egg options:

RAW EGG YOLK

Separate the egg and nestle the raw egg yolk on top of the natto.

RAW EGG YOLK AND FLUFFY EGG WHITE RICE

If you are really into this creamy texture, you can do a little extra thing here, along with the above – whip the white until very fluffy and soft peaks are reached. Stir this though the hot rice with some dashi powder. Yoshie says, the whipped egg white makes the rice 'fuwa fuwa', fluffier and tastier.

FRIED EGG

Simply fry the egg in sesame oil in a hot pan, covered, until you get crisp edges, bright whites and a soft, wobbly egg yolk. Place on top of the natto.

Now dribble over a few extra drops of soy sauce, some spring onions, if you like, and serve immediately.

INGREDIENTS
50 g (1¾ oz) natto (store-bought)
½ teaspoon dashi powder (optional)
1 bowl of freshly steamed Japanese
  short-grain rice (page 80)

TO SERVE
1 very fresh egg (see serving
  suggestions)
1 tablespoon sesame oil
½ teaspoon soy sauce
spring onions (scallions), finely
  chopped (optional)

朝ご

はん

朝お

Scrambled Eggs with Garlic Chives

SERVES 4

ニラ玉

My mother's eyes lit up when she heard I wanted to include these. I admit, they make me very nostalgic too. Garlic chives are not all that easy to find where I live in Tuscany, but occasionally I see large bunches of these at my local Chinese grocer and I snap them up as there is nothing quite like the pungent flavour and crunchy texture of garlic chives. A close substitute would be spring onions (scallions) – just the green part perhaps – or even chives, but you would have to use loads of them to make these, which are practically all garlic chives, held together with a little bit of fluffy egg omelette. These are lovely with a bowl of freshly steamed rice with breakfast, but I also love them on their own as a light lunch or as part of a bigger meal, dressed up a bit with some sesame oil and a few drops of soy sauce or chilli.

69

METHOD

Whisk the eggs together with the water and a good pinch of salt. Set aside.

Chop the garlic chives into 2–3 cm (about 1 in) pieces.

Lightly grease a wide, non-stick frying pan (skillet) with vegetable oil. Over a medium–high heat, stir-fry the garlic chives for 1 minute or until they begin to wilt. Pour over the egg and scramble slightly, shaking the pan so that it covers the whole surface. While it is still quite wobbly, use a spatula to divide the omelette into quarters. Fold in the edges slightly, then flip over each mini-omelette. Cook for 30 more seconds – these should be pale, delicate, fluffy and barely browned.

Serve, garnished as you wish.

INGREDIENTS

3 eggs
1 tablespoon water
a pinch of salt
1 bunch of garlic chives
vegetable oil, for greasing

TO SERVE (OPTIONAL)
a drizzle of sesame oil, a few drops of soy sauce, a sprinkle of sesame seeds, chilli oil or chilli powder

朝ご

Grilled Mochi and Cheese Snack

SERVES 1

磯
辺
餅

This is what I eat when I don't feel like cooking, when I'm hungry but I don't know what I want, when I'm tired, or when I want to treat myself to a moment of comfort. There is a little ritual to making this and when I do it, I think of my mother making these too. I imagine my sister is standing there in the kitchen with me and we are maybe fighting over the last one – or rather, making more so no one has to fight, and laughing about it. It is my instant connection to family members far away.

Kirimochi is a dried rice cake and *isobe* refers to the seaweed – it literally means 'rocky shore'. These dried mochi are a perfect pantry item for times when you want a super-quick, but filling, nourishing snack or meal. Often these are grilled first, then put into soup (an important New Year tradition is clear ozoni soup, where these mochi are the main feature along with vegetables, or you might find them in udon noodle soup, which is known as chikara udon soup), or they are simply boiled.

But I adore these hot, chewy rice cakes grilled most of all, as a savoury snack, but they are equally delicious topped perhaps with Anko (sweet red bean paste, page 234) or with a kinako (roast soybean powder) and sugar coating. My family have always put a thin layer of easily melted cheese onto the top of the mochi, which is a little unusual and perhaps un-Japanese of them, but it works so well.

A word of caution: chew carefully – grilled mochi is incredibly hot and retains its heat very well. My obaachan used to tell me to eat mochi in the winter, because it would keep me warm for hours. She was right, somehow you can feel the heat in your stomach and your mouth long after you've finished it. Not only is mochi hot, even after you've let it rest for a while, but it is very chewy – so what happens is you take a bite, it's so hot and so delicious with that melted cheese and soy sauce, that you chew it too briefly and try to swallow as quickly as you can. It has sadly been known to happen that biting off more mochi than you can chew has led to death by choking. It gives a whole new meaning to your last supper – and, funnily enough, this would probably be mine. So, I repeat, proceed with caution! Chew well and try not to burn yourself.

Cont. >

71

Rice cakes, known as mochi, are not only delightful, but they are one
of the most significant and symbolic Japanese foods. They have been used
in celebrations, especially for the New Year (read more about Osechi
Ryori on page 151), since the 10th century. Like my obaachan encouraging
me to eat warm mochi on a cold day to stay warm, farmers would eat
them in winter to keep their stamina up and it was an easily portable food
for samurai on the battlefield. There are hints at its importance through
the suggestions of where mochi got its name – one idea is from the word *motsu*,
'to hold' or 'to have', as in it is a gift from the deities, or perhaps from
the word *mochizuki*, 'full moon', as mochi rice cakes are traditionally round
and white like a moon.

There is another connection between mochi and the moon. Like most Japanese
children, my mother taught me as a child that the shadows you can see
in the moon are not a man's face, but a rabbit pounding glutinous rice to make
mochi – I still see that rabbit (and only a rabbit) whenever I look up at the
moon and my children do now, too. The 'Tsuki no Usagi' or Rabbit Moon
folktale is based on a Buddhist legend, where the man on the moon
arrives on earth disguised as a beggar. He asks a fox, a monkey and a rabbit
for food. The fox fetches him a fish, the monkey grabs some fruit from
a tree, but the rabbit has only grass, which the man cannot eat. So, he
throws himself on a fire to offer himself to the beggar. Awed by the rabbit's
generosity and sacrifice, the beggar turns back into the man on the moon
and takes the rabbit with him, placing its image in the moon for people
to look up to.

72

METHOD

Place the soy sauce in a small saucer and cut the half sheet of nori in half again
lengthways so you have two long strips.

Heat a dry, heavy frying pan (skillet) over a medium–high heat and place the
blocks of mochi in the pan. Grill them, turning as needed, until the mochi
are browned in spots and puffed up, about 5–6 minutes altogether. They will
appear still dry on the outside and may not be browned all over but only
in parts – the key is that they are puffy. Remove from the heat.

Dip the mochi immediately into the soy sauce, where you will hear a crackle
and pop as you place a piece of cheese on top and wrap in seaweed.
Place the mochi, cheese-side down, on the hot pan again (off the heat) for
a moment until the cheese is melted.

Enjoy immediately. In between bites, you may like to dip the mochi in the
rest of the soy sauce.

INGREDIENTS

1 tablespoon soy sauce
½ sheet of nori seaweed
2 kirimochi (dried mochi blocks)
2 slices of your favourite good melting
    cheese, cut to fit the size of the mochi

朝ご

73

OKOME

お
米

RICE

'Rice is a beautiful food. It is beautiful when it grows – precision rows
of sparkling green stalks shooting up to reach the hot summer sun. It is
beautiful when harvested, autumn gold sheaves piled in diked, patchwork
paddies. It is beautiful when, once threshed, it enters granary bins like a
cataract of tiny seed-pearls. It is beautiful when cooked by a practised hand,
pure white and sweetly fragranced.'

—
SHIZUO TSUJI
in *Japanese Cooking: A Simple Art, 1980*

お

It is an understatement to say rice is the most important dish in Japanese cuisine. It is the very essence of Japanese culture. It is not only the staple dish of every meal, whether humble or formal course-after-course degustation, but rice is also vital for its role in making sake and vinegar, ingredients that are so essential in flavouring dishes and preserving food, such as pickles, and Japanese cuisine wouldn't be what it is without these ingredients. Historically, even outside of the kitchen – as none of the plant was wasted – rice was also important for its use in making paper and glue for books, for fuel, tatami mats and building materials. It was even used like currency.

Japan's available arable land (only about 12 per cent of the country) is a small proportion compared to its mountains and forests, but like a lot of Asia, it has very humid summers and a higher than average rainfall. The wet weather, along with the abundant rivers found running through the mountain ranges, is the perfect climate for wet-rice cultivation, but not without its challenges.

In the foothills of the mountains of Nagano, I visited a village called Sasahara, where I was told about the founders – eleven families, who, almost 400 years ago, cleared the bamboo in the area to create terraces on the land for rice fields in what is known as the 'rice line', a border above which rice does not grow due to the harsh mountain winters. The families bonded together in order to cultivate rice. They diverted mountain rivers into pools to be warmed by the sun before being let out through a hand-dug, kilometres-long water network called segi, in a shared irrigation system to flood the village's rice fields. This sharing of water resources among rice-farming communities was common in Japan and, together with the fact that wet-rice farming was incredibly labour-intensive, meant that living close, working harmoniously together and relying on each other was important to successfully grow and harvest the rice. Each harvest was a joint effort. Each grain of rice a result of the hard work of many.

お米ひと粒に七人の神様が宿っている

'SEVEN GODS LIVE IN ONE GRAIN OF RICE.'

Just like the concept of itadakimasu, the ritual that precedes every meal (see page 11), the phrase you see above teaches gratitude and appreciation of all the challenges, hurdles and hard work that went into growing, harvesting, transporting and cooking the rice that sits in your bowl. Each grain of rice is valuable. It can be disrespectful to leave large amounts of food behind – perhaps that is why portions are small to begin with, so you do not need to waste any food if you cannot finish it. ●

77

お

THE PERFECT BOWL OF JAPANESE RICE

パーフェクトなご飯

A bowl of steamed Japanese rice is quite unlike its equivalent in any other culture. Japan's unique rice cultivar is a soft, short-grain rice; when cooked perfectly, it creates grains that are incredibly moist and stick to each other, which is part of the secret of being able to eat it easily with chopsticks. A bowl of plain Japanese rice is a canvas to the umami-rich sauces and dishes that are eaten with it, but there are also many variations on the regular bowl of rice, usually seasonal. Chestnuts might be cooked together with rice in late autumn (fall), or perhaps fresh peas in the spring and corn in the summer. My grandmother would sometimes cook the rice in fragrant habucha (roasted cassia seed tea) for a rice porridge, a dish that my mother likes if she isn't feeling well.

Often, a plain bowl of hot rice might be served just with a very fresh raw egg yolk and a splash of soy sauce on top, to mix through quickly with chopsticks. When we were children, my mother used to scramble the egg for us with the rice, cooking it a bit like a quick-fried rice. It is still my go-to comfort food and a great way to use up any leftover rice (see Tamago no gohan, page 101).

Although nigiri sushi isn't usually something you would eat at home (my grandmother would order it in from a sushi shop for special occasions), when just-cooked rice is dressed in a sweet rice vinegar it makes a bed for festive and colourful Chirashizushi (page 93), or one of my favourite dinners when I visit my mother – Temaki (hand-rolled sushi, page 97), where a huge bowl of sushi rice accompanies a large platter of favourite fillings, from raw fresh fish or smoked salmon to braised carrots and shiitake mushrooms, rolled omelette and square pieces of dry nori to fit in the palm of your hand. You just fill and eat, as you please.

米

Steamed Rice

SERVES 3–4

ご
は
ん

Although my grandmother and mother have used an electric rice cooker for as long as I can remember, I have had to cook rice on the stove top ever since moving away for university – and I still do. This is, I find, the best way to replicate the soft, moist, sticky rice that comes out perfectly in an electric rice cooker. It is important to have a small, heavy-based saucepan or earthenware pot with a properly fitting lid, because the second part of the cooking process involves steaming and allowing the rice to finish cooking off the heat, covered.

Soaking the rice before cooking also helps to make it that perfectly soft and slightly sticky consistency, but I for one am often guilty of forgetting or running out of time to do it and I can confirm you *can* make a decent pot of rice even when skipping the soaking part, but if you get in the habit of remembering to soak the rice, it'll only be better. One thing you shouldn't forget to do, though, is wash the rice two or three times before cooking. It should always be part of the ritual of cooking rice. You don't even have to throw out all the water – save that starchy 'first wash' from the rice to cook daikon in; it is said to remove the bitterness from the radish and keep it a brilliant white colour.

For perfect rice, just follow a simple ratio: for each portion of rice, use one and a half times the same volume in water. I generally use a ¼-cup measure per person, so a 1-cup measure of rice for the family needs 1½ cups of water. But you could use anything – a yoghurt pot, a smaller cup measure, an espresso cup – whatever it is, just keep that ratio in mind. The traditional Japanese measure is called a gou and is a volume of 180 ml (about ¾ cup), enough for two to three Japanese rice bowls.

Rice does not keep well in the fridge – the grains go unpleasantly hard and any leftover rice kept this way is only good for making Fried rice (page 102), omuraisu (rice omelette) or Tamago no gohan (page 101) the next day, so unless I know I will be making any of those dishes, I usually make only as much as I need to serve it warm. If you do have leftovers, freeze them in portions. With this method of cooking on the stove top, you can cook even the smallest amount, for one, if you like, but do keep in mind that you will get a better result with a fuller pot, so use a small one for a small amount.

This quantity is just right for three or four small Japanese rice bowls. If you are making a donburi bowl, or are simply a rice lover, you may want to double the amount.

80

お

METHOD

Place the rice in a small, deep, heavy-based pan with a tight-fitting lid. Fill with cool water and wash the rice, swirling it with your hand several times. Drain (keep the water for boiling vegetables), then repeat the washing 2–3 more times. Ideally, let it soak for 30 minutes at this point, if you can.

Drain the rice and re-fill the saucepan with the measured cool, fresh water. Set over a low–medium heat on your smallest hob, bring to a simmer, then turn the heat down to the lowest setting, cover with the lid and cook for about 10–12 minutes, or up to 15 minutes. Lifting the lid for a peek will let out much of the desired steam so it is best to avoid this (a well-trained ear can hear when the water has been almost completely absorbed). That said, do keep an eye on it if it is your first time trying this method, as individual stove heats and pan materials do indeed make a difference to cooking rice – at the slightest hint of the rice burning or the water evaporating too quickly, take it off the heat and let it finish cooking by steaming. If you taste the rice at this point it should be just very slightly al dente, still quite moist but not mushy. Turn off the heat, keep the lid on and leave to steam for 10 minutes.

Fluff the warm rice with a rice paddle and serve immediately.

INGREDIENTS

200 g (1 cup) Japanese short-grain rice
375 ml (1½ cups) cool water

Filled Rice Balls

MAKES 4

お
に
ぎ
り

INGREDIENTS

60 g (2 oz) smoked salmon
vegetable oil, for cooking (optional)
2 cups freshly cooked, still warm
 Japanese short-grain rice (page 80)
1 spring onion (scallion), finely chopped
salt, as needed
1 tablespoon toasted sesame seeds
1 umeboshi (pickled plum), pitted and
 split in half
2 sheets of nori, cut in half (optional)

One night, while up very late talking with my mother, we started making onigiri for a picnic the next day with the kids, her grandchildren. Onigiri is something that children love, that everyone loves, as they make possibly the most perfect portable food or a snack on the run for a lunchbox, a picnic or a train ride. I watched my mother shape them in her hands – she rubbed a pinch of salt on them so the rice wouldn't stick, cupped the onigiri, pressing with both hands, firmly but not too much – just right. Onigiri comes from the words, *o*, meaning 'giving honour' and *nigiri*, 'to grasp'. This is more than just a ball of rice. I remember being told that in the act of making onigiri, you transmit your love through your hands into the rice for the person you are making it for. I was watching my mother do just that that night.

Onigiri is shaped into a little triangle of rice that is seasoned with anything you want – it can even be left plain! My favourites are also classics: salmon (leftover Grilled salmon, page 59, would be perfect, but if you don't have any handy then some lightly cooked smoked salmon is a great replacement), sesame and umeboshi (pickled plums). If umeboshi has too much of a kick for you, you can simply leave it out or make your own onigiri with whatever foods you have around, even a little ball of tinned tuna mixed with some Japanese mayonnaise in the centre is very good. You can also mix things into the rice: cooked peas, corn or edamame, for example. If you like, you can wrap nori around the onigiri so you don't get your hands sticky when eating them. If you aren't serving them immediately, though, pack the nori separately so that the seaweed will remain nice and crisp.

METHOD

Quickly cook the smoked salmon in a non-stick or lightly oiled pan until opaque, pale and almost crumbly, about 3 minutes. Place in a bowl and mix with half of the rice, along with the spring onion.

With wet hands, take a pinch of salt and rub it over your hands. Pick up about half of the salmon-rice mixture and firmly cup in both of your hands to give it a firm triangle shape with no loose rice. Set down and repeat so that you have two salmon onigiri. If you find any rice is sticking to your hands, wet them again and rub a pinch of salt back over your hands.

Stir the sesame seeds through the remaining rice until well distributed. Wet and salt your hands as before, take half of the sesame-rice and place half an umeboshi in the middle of the rice before cupping in your hands to shape into a triangle. Repeat with the rest of the rice and the rest of the umeboshi.

The onigiri can be enjoyed as they are, or placed in a bento box to be eaten later that day. You can also pack them with a piece of nori (split a large sheet in half so you have two long pieces about 10 cm/4 in wide and use these to wrap around the whole onigiri), which helps to make eating them less sticky.

お

Kakinohazushi (persimmon-leaf sushi, page 86)

お

A BRIEF HISTORY
OF SUSHI

寿
司
の
歴
史

One of the most famous dishes of Japanese cuisine, sushi in Japan generally refers to nigiri sushi (or nigirizushi, note that the 's' becomes a 'z' sound when it goes behind another word), which is a mound of rice smeared with some wasabi and topped with a piece of raw, marinated or sometimes cooked seafood or rolled egg omelette (page 61). This is undoubtedly the most revered form of sushi, and the most expensive, too. Sushi in a roll form is usually called makizushi and includes Futomaki (page 89), a thick, colourful roll of rice and many vegetables and fish wrapped inside nori seaweed.

Sushi was introduced to Japan from China, probably in the 8th century, although the preparation can be traced back to more than 2,000 years ago. It originated in narezushi, a dish of fish fermented with salt and rice, often for months, and that is similar to preparations found in South-East Asian countries. But with this kind of sushi, it was only the fish that was eaten, the fermented rice was discarded. Between the 14th and 16th centuries a new style of sushi, namanare, emerged, with a shorter period of fermentation, then by the 18th century in the Edo period, the fermented rice disappeared altogether and was replaced with vinegared rice. This version, known as hayazushi, became completely unique to Japanese culture: rice, mixed with sweetened vinegar, served with fish, vegetables and dried ingredients.

Each region of Japan produces a variety of sushi styles with local ingredients that have been passed down for generations. For example, Kakinohazushi (pictured opposite), which developed in landlocked Nara in the Edo period, and is known today for being a wonderfully portable sushi, the kind you can buy at a bento box shop at train stations to take on the shinkansen. Instead of being wrapped in seaweed, the rice and fish is wrapped in persimmon leaves, which aren't eaten, but due to their natural antibacterial properties are perfect for preserving the fish and rice for hours, even days.

Then you have makizushi, a sushi roll wrapped in seaweed. With the invention of the sheet form of nori around 1750, the makizushi rolled style of sushi emerged. Current day makizushi first appeared in a culinary book in 1776, *Shinsen Kondate Buruishū,* which gives the following directions: 'Place a sheet of asakusa-nori, pufferfish skin or paper on the makisu and spread the cooked rice, then arrange the fish on it. Roll the makisu tightly from one side...' Today, most makizushi uses nori as the outer layer, although there are many regional variations.

Also in the Edo period, around the 1820s or '30s, came the rise of a popular fast food invented in Edo (Tokyo): nigirizushi. One common origin story suggests that the chef Hanaya Yohei (1799–1858) was the one to invent, or at least perfect, the nigirizushi technique in 1824, at his shop in Ryōgoku. After the Great Kanto Earthquake in 1923, nigirizushi chefs were displaced from Edo throughout Japan, popularising the dish throughout the country. ●

米

Persimmon-Leaf Sushi

MAKES 12 PIECES

柿
の
葉
寿
司

In Kyoto or Tokyo, you might notice this persimmon-leaf sushi in the shops selling bento boxes for the shinkansen, the bullet train. It's because it is the perfect travelling food. I first read about this preparation in Jun'ichirō Tanizaki's *In Praise of Shadows*, a 1933 essay on Japanese aesthetics in a fast-changing world. It's not a cookbook (he discusses things like electricity and the treatment of the elderly), but he includes a detailed recipe for this persimmon-leaf sushi from a friend who had been to the mountainous region of Yoshino in Nara prefecture, which – he writes – is 'far better than the sushi one gets in Tokyo. I became so fond of it that I ate almost nothing else this summer... The oil of the salmon and the slight hint of salt give just the proper touch of seasoning to the rice, and the salmon becomes as soft as if it were fresh.'

Tanizaki describes not only the proportions of sake to rice, and the position of the leaf when rolling the sushi, but describes how the sushi must be packed so that no space remains between them, before a heavy stone is placed on top, as in making pickles.

Kakinohazushi has its origins in the Edo period in landlocked Nara, where it originated as a way to transport fish without the use of modern refrigeration. Persimmon leaves – naturally antibacterial and full of tannins that help preserve the fish and rice – take the place of seaweed, and some recipes for this dish include lake trout rather than saltwater fish, although it's commonly now seen with salmon or mackerel. What also makes this sushi different is that it doesn't have the classic vinegar dressing and the fish isn't just raw and fresh, it is often salted or marinated in some vinegar and then moulded in the hand with salt, 'the secret being that only salt should touch the rice'. All of this – the salt, the persimmon leaves, the seasoning of the fish – is meant to ensure it stays edible for many hours, and is therefore a lot more portable than regular sushi, which can only be eaten very fresh. It is usually prepared in the evening for the next day.

The mother of my good friend Junko Mizoguchi makes this with smoked salmon, a very good way to make this easily at home, as long as you can get fresh persimmon leaves – choose ones that are whole, free of holes and about as large as the palm of your hand.

86

お

METHOD

Wash the rice in cold water 2–3 times, swirling the rice with your hands and then draining each time, until the excess starch is washed off. Place in a small–medium heavy-based pan that has a lid along with the measured water and bring to a simmer over a medium heat. Add the sake to the pan but do not stir it in, cover with a tight-fitting lid and reduce the heat to as low as you can. Cook for 15–17 minutes, or until all the liquid has been absorbed and the rice is tender. Remove from the heat and keep the lid on until the rice has cooled.

In the meantime, prepare the persimmon leaves. Rinse them one by one, front and back, then bring a small pan of water to the boil. Add a generous three-fingered pinch of coarse salt, then blanch the leaves for 30 seconds. Remove and lay out on a clean dish towel to dry them. Rub the surface gently with another dish towel to ensure they are clean and dry and snip off any stems with a pair of scissors. Blanching the leaves helps to make them soft enough to roll neatly.

Cut the smoked salmon into 12 even, rectangular pieces, roughly 6 cm × 3 cm (2½ in × 1¼ in) in size.

Now to shape. Although Tanizaki warns against the presence of any moisture, I find the only way for the rice not to stick to your hands is to begin with wet hands, like when making onigiri. Shake off any excess water, then dip your finger into the salt and rub it all over your hands. Take a scoop of rice, about the size of a large walnut, or 30 g (1oz), and shape into a firm log, the size of three fingers, about 6 cm × 3 cm (2½ in × 1¼ in). Use both hands to cup the rice and squeeze it together so no rice is loose. Make 12 of these – you won't need to wet your hands each time, but you should always salt them and you will see that after making several of these salt alone is enough to prevent the rice from sticking. If it does, wet them again, but don't forget the salt.

Place a piece of salmon over the top of each piece of rice. Take a clean, dry, blanched persimmon leaf, shiny side up, place the sushi at the stem end and roll up, tucking in the tip underneath. Alternatively, if you have narrow or smaller leaves, place the sushi, fish-side down at the widest part of the leaf (usually the centre) and roll the rest of the leaf around it. Place the finished pieces with the tips underneath in a small dish or container, side by side. Once done, place a sheet of baking paper or aluminium foil over the top and rest a weight on top. Press the sushi like this for at least 1 hour and up to 12 hours, at room temperature. Note that sushi should never be refrigerated.

To eat, unwrap the persimmon leaf and eat only the sushi, not the leaf. It makes the perfect travel food, because you won't get your hands sticky and you don't even need a plate – the leaf takes care of all of that for you.

INGREDIENTS

200 g (1 cup) Japanese short-grain rice
375 ml (1½ cups) water
1 tablespoon sake
12 persimmon leaves
150 g (5½ oz) smoked salmon

お

Sushi Rolls

MAKES 4 SUSHI ROLLS
(6–8 PIECES PER ROLL)

Futomaki is one of those things that is brought to parties or picnics and that everyone loves for its colours and flavours. It is more often home-made, unlike nigirizushi, which is usually eaten in a sushi shop. Each household has their own favourite sushi fillings; these are mine, although my mother often includes strips of blanched spinach, too, for extra colour (you could use about 5–10 strips for a large futomaki roll). Feel free to add any of these other popular ingredients: kanpyo (gourd strips), ginger pickles, strips of pickled daikon (the bright yellow takuan pickle), tofu, crabmeat, cooked prawns (shrimp), raw tuna or salmon sashimi, cut into strips, or avocado. You could also use ready-made sushizu (sushi vinegar), but if you don't have it, you can find the recipe below.

METHOD

Wash the rice in cold water 2–3 times, swirling the rice with your hands and then draining each time, until the excess starch is washed off. Place in a small, heavy-based pan that has a tight-fitting lid along with the measured water. Cover and bring to a gentle simmer over a low heat, then cook for 15 minutes, or until the water seems all absorbed. Remove from the heat and keep the lid on, allowing the rice to steam for a further 15 minutes.

For the sushizu, heat the vinegar, sugar and salt in a small saucepan until dissolved – do not let it boil. Set aside (this will keep in a jar in the fridge for 3 weeks if not using immediately).

When ready to dress the warm rice, place in a wide and shallow bowl (even better, a handai – a special Japanese rice bowl, which is made of cypress wood and absorbs excess moisture), pour over about ¼ cup (or to taste) of the sushizu for the above amount of cooked rice and mix through using a spatula in a cutting motion so you do not squash the rice grains. It helps to fan it while doing this to help extra moisture evaporate, until the rice has cooled slightly. It is important not to squash the rice while doing this, or make it soggy with the added vinegar, so it is useful to do this with an extra set of hands: one of you fans the rice, while the other carefully distributes the vinegar and turns the rice over so it has a chance to cool.

Sushi rice should be body temperature when making sushi. The number one rule is *never* put it in the fridge, the grains go very hard and the texture will be ruined.

For the marinated vegetables, remove the shiitake mushrooms from their soaking liquid (reserve the liquid). Slice off the stems and slice the caps thinly. Place in a small saucepan along with the carrot sticks, soy sauce and sugar, then add enough of the shiitake soaking water (filtered through a tea strainer, if necessary) to cover. Simmer until the liquid is reduced and the vegetables are very soft, about 15 minutes. Drain and set aside.

Cont. >

INGREDIENTS

89

RICE
300 g (1½ cups) Japanese
   short-grain rice
430 ml (1¾ cups) water

SUSHIZU
125 ml (½ cup) rice vinegar
3 tablespoons sugar
3 teaspoons salt

MARINATED VEGETABLES
6–8 dried shiitake mushrooms, soaked
   in hot water for 20 minutes
1 carrot, peeled and cut into sticks
1 tablespoon soy sauce
1 tablespoon sugar

ROLLS
4–8 leaves of butter lettuce or shiso
1 × Tamagoyaki roll (page 61), cut
   into strips
1 cucumber, seeded and sliced
   lengthways into sticks
4 sheets of nori

TO SERVE
soy sauce
wasabi
Gari (pickled ginger, page 35)

SHAPING THE SUSHI

Nori has a smooth side and a slightly rough side. Place the smooth side face-down on a bamboo rolling mat. Spread the sushi rice over the entire sheet of nori (about 1 cm/½ in thick), leaving just the top 2 cm (¾ in) of the seaweed and the bottom 5 mm (¼ in) bare. The rice should go all the way to the edges to the left and right.

Add your fillings in a line running left to right in the centre of the nori. You can choose any combination of fillings. If using leafy greens like shiso or lettuce, I like to lay these down first and then lay the other fillings on top.

Now you have to simultaneously hold the nori to the bamboo mat with your fingers and carefully roll the mat towards the top, using your middle, ring and pinky fingers to hold in the fillings as you roll over – all while keeping the roll tight. As you reach the end of the nori sheet, make sure to lift out the bamboo mat so that the nori is adhered to itself. Use the mat to help tighten and shape the roll. Don't squeeze too hard, but while the bamboo mat is still around the roll, you can use this as an opportunity to check that the filling is centred and everything looks good. It sounds harder than it is!

Once you have rolled the nori well, unroll the mat and place the sushi roll on a chopping board. Wet your sharpest, large kitchen knife with a damp cloth and cut your roll in half. Wipe the knife again to remove any traces of rice, then cut each half into three or four pieces, according to how thick you would like them. For large futomaki, I usually cut them into eight pieces so that the pieces are not too huge; for smaller rolls, they can be longer pieces, so I cut into six.

Serve with a small dish of soy sauce, a dab of wasabi and gari on the side to cleanse the palate.

90

A NOTE ON SOY SAUCE

Don't use too much soy sauce when enjoying sushi, it's a mistake I often see people making outside of Japan. You don't need to flood your dish with soy sauce. What will happen is that when you go to dip, the sushi becomes so soaked with sauce that first of all, it falls apart, and secondly, the rice soaks up too much and is much too salty. If you only have the tiniest amount of soy sauce in your dish, you can avoid all of that happening and you can easily top up if you want more.

お

米

お

No one I know makes nigari sushi at home, it is something that is only eaten out – or ordered from a sushi shop and enjoyed at home that way. Chirashizushi is a 'scattered sushi', which has the flavours of your favourite box of nigari sushi, but is not only easy to make at home, it is a very fun, colourful and festive meal – perfect for celebrations and get togethers at home. It is a family-friendly dish in Japan and is often the star of the table along with Ichigo daifuku (strawberry-filled mochi, page 243) for festive days like Hinamatsuri (Girls' Day), a centuries-old festival that is celebrated on March 3, and Kodomo no hi (Children's Day) on May 5.

Obaachan would usually make chirashizushi with cooked prawns (shrimp), snow peas (mangetout), egg strips, kanpyo (dried gourd strips) and fresh bamboo shoots in the spring. My mother recalls it never had sashimi in it, as you commonly see today. You can easily substitute different vegetables and fish here, but the idea is to make a very colourful dish, so be aware of the different colours and balance those out. Use greens such as peas or spinach. Bamboo shoots, kanpyo and aburaage (fried beancurd) are also very traditional additions that have a wonderful texture and flavour here. You could also use kingfish, tuna or salmon roe, which is popular, for a pretty pop of colour. Or leave the raw fish off completely if you want a dish that is easier to keep.

Scattered Sushi

SERVES 4

ちらし寿司

93

METHOD

For the sushi rice, first wash the rice in cold water 2–3 times, then place in a small pot with the measured water, cover and bring to a gentle simmer over a low heat. Cook for 15 minutes, or until the water seems all absorbed, then remove from the heat. Keep the lid on, and allow the rice to steam for a further 15 minutes.

INGREDIENTS

SUSHI RICE
300 g (1½ cups) Japanese
  short-grain rice
430 ml (1¾ cups) water

SUSHI VINEGAR
60 ml (¼ cup) rice vinegar
3 tablespoons sugar
3 teaspoons salt

TOPPING
6–8 dried shiitake mushrooms, soaked
  in hot water for 20 minutes
1 carrot, peeled and cut into sticks
1 tablespoon soy sauce
1½ tablespoons sugar
120 g (4½ oz) lotus root, an 8 cm (3 in)
  piece, peeled and thinly sliced
85 g (3 oz) edamame in their pods
3 eggs
¼ teaspoon salt
vegetable oil, for greasing
150 g (5 ½ oz) prawns (shrimp)
150 g (5 ½ oz) sushi-grade raw salmon,
  diced into 1 cm (½ in) cubes

For the sushi vinegar, heat the rice vinegar, sugar and salt in a small saucepan until dissolved – do not let it boil. Set aside (this will keep in a jar in the fridge for 3 weeks, if not using right away). Reserve a little of the vinegar mixture to season the lotus root with. When ready to dress the warm rice, pour over bit by bit (up to ¼ cup or to taste – the dressing should coat the rice enough to make it shiny and tasty, but not soggy) and mix through using a spatula in a cutting motion, so you do not squash the rice grains. It helps to fan the rice while doing this, or until it has cooled slightly. As with the futomaki, it is important that the sushi rice should be at room temperature – do not put it in the fridge, the grains go very hard and the texture will be ruined. You can make this seasoned rice several hours ahead of time; the vinegar helps the rice keep well.

Remove the shiitake mushrooms from their soaking liquid (reserve the liquid). Remove and discard the stems and slice the rest of the mushroom thinly. Place them in a small saucepan along with the carrot sticks, soy sauce and 1 tablespoon of the sugar, then add enough of the shiitake soaking water (filtered through a tea strainer, if necessary) to cover. Simmer until the liquid is reduced and the vegetables are very soft, about 15 minutes. Drain and set aside.

Boil the lotus root slices for about 2 minutes. Lift them out of the water, then sprinkle with some of the sushi vinegar to season. Set aside.

Boil the edamame in the same water until tender – about 5 minutes if cooking from frozen; 2 minutes if fresh. Drain and plunge into a bowl of ice-cold water to stop the cooking and keep the colour bright. Pod them and set the beans aside.

Beat the eggs with the remaining 2 teaspoons of sugar and the salt. Heat a non-stick frying pan (skillet) over a medium–high heat and lightly grease with oil, wiping away any excess. Ladle about a third of the egg mixture into the pan and swirl to distribute the egg – you are making a very thin, pale egg crepe. It only needs about 1 minute and you do not need to flip, the surface should look dry. Continue with the rest of the batter to make 3 crêpes in total. Slice each into thin strips and set aside.

The prawns should be cleaned – remove heads and the central digestive tract that you can often see as a dark line. I like to keep the tails on, but you can remove these too, if you like. Boil for 1 minute, or until they turn opaque. Set aside.

To assemble, place the seasoned, cooled sushi rice in the bottom of a large bowl (alternatively, you can do these in individual bowls). Mix through about half of the vegetables and prawns until evenly incorporated. Scatter the rest of the vegetables on top, followed by the egg strips and, finally, top attractively with the remaining prawns and salmon. Enjoy immediately.

米

お

Hand-Rolled Sushi

SERVES 4

手
巻
き
寿
司

Along with the Sukiyaki (page 177), this is the dish I request most from my mother when I visit her. Like the chirashizushi, it is what more closely resembles sushi made at home – except that instead of rolling the sushi or preparing nigiri, you simply lay out all the ingredients in pretty platters, have a plate of nori cut into squares and a large bowl of sushi rice and everyone rolls their own sushi. What I love so much about it is that it is so interactive and it's the perfect meal to share with family members or a group of friends. I particularly appreciate this as my children can choose what they want in their sushi, which is different from what I want in mine, and it's less work for the cook, who can actually be at the table with everyone – ideal for a get-together, if you ask me. For a vegetarian version, replace the seafood with the marinated shiitake and carrot from the Futomaki recipe (page 89) and feel free to add any other favourite vegetables – some blanched green beans or asparagus are also the perfect size and shape.

97

METHOD

Set the table with a small plate for each person, a small shallow bowl for soy sauce (see my note on soy sauce, page 90) and an optional dab of wasabi in each bowl. You might like to put out a small dish of pickled ginger to cleanse the palate between rolls.

Place the sushi rice in a large bowl with a serving paddle. Put the nori sheets in a pile on a small plate. Arrange a platter with all the fillings nicely and neatly laid out.

Guests make their own temaki sushi by taking a square of nori in their palm. Add a small amount of rice and flatten it a little. Place your preferred fillings – pick three or four, not too many at once – on the diagonal and fold the edges in so you have a cone-shape. Dip briefly in the soy sauce and eat! The beauty of this is that you can make as many as you like and use whatever combination of fillings for each one.

INGREDIENTS

1 × quantity cooked sushi rice
  (page 87)
5–10 sheets of nori, cut into quarters
  (scissors work best, or fold and tear)
1 × Tamagoyaki (rolled egg omelette,
  page 61), cut into strips about the
  length of your palm
cucumber, cut into thin sticks
avocado, cut into thin wedges
fresh shiso leaves (or some butter
  lettuce or other green salad leaf)
450 g (1 lb) raw, sashimi-grade seafood,
  for example: prawns (shrimp), salmon,
  tuna, sea bream, scallops

SERVE
soy sauce
wasabi
Gari (pickled ginger, page 35)

米

お

This is the dish I request most
from my mother when I visit her.
What I love so much about
it is that it is so interactive and
it's the perfect meal to share
with family or friends; it's less work
for the cook, who can actually
be at the table with everyone –
ideal for a get-together, if you ask me.

米

お

Egg and Rice

卵
の
ご
飯

This is pure comfort food for me, the dish that sends me right back to my childhood, and the thing I make when I am not feeling well or want to eat something but don't feel like cooking. It's also become a dish that my children request often, and I love that it has become a family tradition. This is essentially a cooked version of tamago no gohan, also known as tamago kake gohan, which is normally made with raw egg mixed through hot rice with a splash of soy sauce. Like Yoshie's Natto (page 66), the key to the raw version is the mixing of the raw egg through the hot rice to create a silky, creamy consistency. It's wonderful. But if raw egg isn't for you, then try this cooked version, which takes only one pan and one minute longer than the raw version. The cooked version makes excellent use of leftover rice.

101

METHOD

This is very quick to cook, so have everything ready.

Using a fork or chopsticks, beat the egg together with the soy sauce until well combined.

Grease a frying pan (skillet) with just enough oil to cover and wipe off any excess with some kitchen paper. Heat until hot, then pour over the egg mixture, which should immediately start bubbling, and scramble it for a brief moment. While everything is still very custardy and wobbly, tip over the rice and spread it out so that it gets soaked in the egg. Now just toss the mixture like you would fried rice until the egg is cooked to your liking – you really only need 1 minute or so. I like to use a spatula for this, or chopsticks. I do think the beauty in this comforting dish is the fact that it is so simple (any more and it becomes fried rice like the Chahan on page 102), but you could add a sprinkling of dashi powder to the egg, or some Furikake (page 31) to the top of the rice when serving (my youngest likes it this way).

INGREDIENTS

PER PERSON
1 egg
1 teaspoon soy sauce
vegetable oil, for greasing
1 bowl of cooked Japanese rice
  (page 80), warm or cold

米

Fried Rice

SERVES 4 GENEROUSLY

チ
ャ
ー
ハ
ン

Much like Tamago no gohan (page 101), this is a great way to use up any leftover rice – and, in fact, day-old rice is even better suited to this dish than freshly cooked rice – indeed any leftover fish, meat or vegetables even. The idea here is really to use whatever you might have in the fridge; typically I go for four or five ingredients. Spring onions (scallions) are a must for their flavour, but if you don't have them then half an onion will do. There's usually something green, like green beans, peas, snow peas (mangetout), edamame or some spinach. Carrot or mushrooms, even rehydrated shiitake mushrooms if you don't have fresh ones, are great. You can also add leftover salted grilled fish (page 59), prawns (shrimp), chicken or ham. Even tinned corn. And if you don't have much at all in the fridge, even just spring onions and egg (so a step up from the tamago no gohan) or some fish like salmon is perfect. Whatever needs to be cooked ahead can be cooked separately and set aside (like the egg, below) and whatever is already cooked can be added at the end along with the egg just until combined. If you have it, shiso leaf is wonderful to garnish, lending a fresh flavour that lifts everything.

102

INGREDIENTS

1 tablespoon vegetable oil
2 eggs, beaten
4 fresh shiitake (or button) mushrooms, finely chopped
2 spring onions (scallions), white parts finely sliced; green parts sliced on the diagonal
a handful of green beans, chopped
a generous pinch of salt
4 cups cooked, cold rice (day-old is fine) (page 80)
3 teaspoons soy sauce
1 shiso leaf, thinly sliced (optional)
drizzle of sesame oil

METHOD

Heat half of the vegetable oil in a good, non-stick frying pan (skillet) or wok over a medium heat and scramble the eggs for about 1 minute or so until pale, fluffy and just cooked. Set aside.

Add the rest of the oil to the pan and cook the mushrooms and the white parts of the onions together with the beans and salt. Cook for 2–3 minutes, or until the beans are tender. Add the rice and break it up with a spatula – especially important if the rice is cold. Toss everything together to combine and to warm up the rice, about 2 minutes. Add the soy sauce, quickly followed by the reserved egg, breaking it up with the spatula. As soon as it is all combined well, take off the heat and serve the rice with the green parts of the onions scattered over the top, followed by the shiso, if using, and a drizzle of sesame oil.

お

Braised Beef Bowl

牛
丼

Donburi are comforting, casual dishes served in a large soup bowl (in fact, donburi is the name of this particular bowl), not the standard-sized Japanese rice bowl. They call for a larger amount of rice and a quickly cooked topping, usually meat, with a very juicy, delicious sauce around it that gets soaked into the rice – the sauce is fundamental. Donburi are often just eaten on their own as they are quite filling, but if you want something to go with this, I love a side of pickled vegetables to nibble and brighten the meal.

Gyudon is a brilliantly quick beef rice bowl, where the beef and onion are flavoured with a sweet soy sauce much like a sukiyaki sauce. As you will read on page 16, Japan has a very long history of not eating red meat and it is still consumed in relatively smaller portions. For me this donburi is all about the sauce and the rice. If you feel this is a too-small amount of meat, you are welcome to double it, although I think with a few pickles or some of the side dishes in the vegetable chapter, and perhaps an egg on top, it makes an extremely satisfying meal. There are a couple of variations where you could finish with an egg on top (I will always say yes to an egg on top): tsukimi gyudon, my personal favourite, is with a very fresh raw egg yolk – as you mix it into the hot dish, the egg yolk coats everything, making a rich and creamy sauce; tanindon is where you add beaten egg just at the last minute of the cooking as the beef is braising in its sauce – it is a similar preparation to oyakodon, another popular donburi, or rice bowl, with chicken and egg; or you can add a poached egg on top.

103

METHOD

To make the sauce, place the ingredients in a small saucepan and warm, stirring occasionally, until the sugar has dissolved. Set aside.

Heat the oil in a frying pan (skillet) over a medium heat, then cook the onion, stirring, until beginning to get transparent, about 2–3 minutes – add a splash of water if you see it in danger of browning. Add the beef and continue cooking for another 2 minutes, or until no longer pink. Pour over the sauce and simmer for a further minute, then remove from the heat.

Top the cooked rice bowls evenly with the beef, pour over the sauce and sprinkle over scallion and beni shoga, if you like. Serve immediately.

VARIATION

Replacing the beef with thinly sliced king trumpet (also known as king brown) mushrooms makes a wonderful vegan/vegetarian version.

INGREDIENTS

1 tablespoon vegetable oil
1 brown (yellow) onion, thinly sliced
300 g (10½ oz) very thinly sliced beef
  (chuck or rib-eye)
4 large bowls of freshly cooked
  Japanese rice (page 80)
1 spring onion (scallion), finely chopped
Beni shoga (red pickled ginger,
  page 36) (optional)

SUKIYAKI SAUCE
2 tablespoons mirin
2 tablespoons sake
2 tablespoons soy sauce
2 tablespoons water
½ tablespoon sugar (or to taste)

米

Shiitake and Chicken Rice

SERVES 4

炊
き
込
み
ご
飯

I absolutely love this way of cooking rice, where you simply put all the ingredients into the one pot together, so the rice absorbs all the flavours and the chicken comes out incredibly tender. It is my ideal comfort food, both to prepare and to eat, as it so easy to do both! Literally meaning 'cooked with rice', you can actually put anything you like in this – it is usually a dish where you might find many autumnal (fall) vegetables like mushrooms and chestnuts, as it's a favourite to make with shinmai (new season rice), which is harvested in the autumn. Although I find it hard to go past this classic shiitake and chicken combination, you could use aburaage or fried beancurd, bamboo shoots, clams or gobo (burdock root – although it can be hard to find outside of Japan). For a bit of richness, add a knob of butter before mixing it all together. To make this vegetarian/vegan, simply omit the chicken and perhaps add a few more different mushrooms or another favourite vegetable. Any leftovers are great turned into Onigiri (page 82).

104

INGREDIENTS

4 dried shiitake mushrooms
250 ml (1 cup) water
1 × 5 cm (2 in) square piece of kombu
2 chicken thighs, deboned and cut into bite-sized pieces
1 tablespoon soy sauce
1 tablespoon mirin
1 tablespoon sake
1 tablespoon minced fresh root ginger
230 g (generous 1 cup) Japanese short-grain rice
½ carrot, peeled and cut into matchsticks
1 spring onion (scallion), green parts finely chopped

METHOD

Soak the mushrooms for at least 1 hour in the water with the kombu. This will make a delicious shiitake dashi that the rice is going to be cooked in. Remove and discard the stem of the rehydrated shiitake mushrooms and finely slice the rest. Set aside. Marinate the chicken in the soy sauce, mirin, sake and ginger for the same time.

Wash and drain the rice two or three times. Drain it very well the last time, then place the rice in a medium heavy-based saucepan with a tight-fitting lid. The key to this dish is in the layering. Add the carrot (or any root vegetables you might be adding) first on top of the rice, followed by the chicken pieces, all their marinade, and the mushrooms. Add the shiitake dashi (remove the kombu and use it in Furikake, page 31). Cover with the lid, bring to the boil, then reduce the heat to very low and cook for 15–17 minutes, or until the liquid has all been absorbed (never touching the rice or ingredients). Let it rest, lid on, for a further 15 minutes to finish steaming.

To serve, toss everything together in the pot and sprinkle over the chopped spring onion.

お

米

Salmon Donburi

SERVES 4

鮭
丼

Like the Gyudon (page 103), this donburi is also filling and quick to prepare, even more so as there is no cooking involved other than the rice. It always satisfies my cravings for sashimi – in fact, you could put whatever ultra-fresh, sashimi-grade seafood you like on this – scallop, scampi or sea urchins are some very luxurious and delicious options. The thing that I think really makes this so good is the sauce (a good donburi has a sauce that flavours the rice underneath), which you could liberally drizzle all over the dish or you could marinate the salmon in it for a bit before assembling.

INGREDIENTS

320–400 g (11½–14 oz) sushi-grade
  raw salmon or other seafood
4 large bowls of freshly cooked rice
  (page 80)
1 sheet of nori, snipped into thin strips
  with scissors
2–4 tablespoons Gari (pickled ginger,
  page 35)
some fresh green vegetables, such as
  thinly sliced cucumbers, avocado,
  blanched green beans, mustard
  greens, rocket (arugula) or finely
  chopped chives

SAUCE
1 tablespoon soy sauce
2 teaspoons mirin
a pinch of sugar

METHOD

Finely cut the fish against the grain in 3–5 mm (¼ in) thick slices. Arrange them on top of the bowls of warm rice along with the nori, pickled ginger and vegetables. Mix together the sauce ingredients until the sugar is dissolved, then sprinkle it over the donburi and enjoy immediately.

米

Mapo Tofu Bowl

SERVES 4

マ
ー
ボ
ー
丼

108

INGREDIENTS

1 teaspoon potato starch or cornflour (corn starch)
1 tablespoon sesame oil
200 g (7 oz) minced (ground) pork
1 knob of ginger, about 3 cm (1¼ in), minced
1 garlic clove, minced
3–4 spring onions (scallions), white and green parts separated and finely chopped
a pinch of salt
80 ml (⅓ cup) sake or Chinese rice wine
1 tablespoon red or brown miso
2 teaspoons doubanjiang (chilli bean sauce)
250 ml (1 cup) stock (any that you have, or water)
250 g (9 oz) tofu (I prefer a medium-firm tofu), diced
4 bowls of cooked rice (page 80)

I have a soft spot for mapo tofu, as I grew up in Beijing where Sichuan restaurants abound and this has always been a dish I have loved. It is much-loved in Japan, too. In fact, it is so popular it is usually just cooked from a special packet mix found in Japanese supermarkets – a bit like Japanese curry, add the meat and tofu and that's it. Mapo tofu was introduced to Japan in the 1950s by Japanese-Chinese chef Chin Kenmin, who is credited with having brought his native Sichuan cuisine to Japanese palates through his restaurant and numerous television shows – his son is chef Chen Kenichi, a.k.a. Iron Chef Chinese from the iconic *Iron Chef* series.

It's not unusual to find adored Chinese dishes that have been borrowed and adapted to Japanese tastes over the centuries – some of the dishes include gyoza (jiǎozi) and ramen (lāmiàn). In the Japanese version, it is more or less a matter of what is in your average Japanese pantry. Less (or sometimes no) doubanjiang (chilli bean sauce) is used (but feel free to add more according to your taste – it is fiery!), there is no douchi (fermented black beans or black bean sauce) or numbing Sichuan pepper (admittedly, it is the thing that makes a mapo tofu, but it is also often the first ingredient omitted for non-Sichuanese tastes) and instead miso is added. This is one of the rare occasions where I prefer red miso for this, it is punchier and stronger in flavour. I prefer a firmer tofu, but the more delicate silken tofu is often used. One thing is for sure, that mapo tofu is perfectly suited to becoming a donburi dish, because the sauce – that ever-important sauce – that seeps into the deep bowl of rice is what makes this dish so very comforting.

You can also use minced (ground) beef or chicken instead of pork. For a vegetarian version, try this with diced eggplant (aubergine) – look for long, thin Japanese or Chinese eggplants to use in place of the meat, they may take 5–10 minutes to cook in the first step.

METHOD

Mix the potato starch with a couple of tablespoons of water to make a slurry. Set aside.

Heat the oil in a cast-iron or heavy-based frying pan (skillet) or wok over a medium–high heat, add the pork, ginger, garlic and the white parts of the spring onion, along with a good pinch of salt. Stir-fry for 2–3 minutes, or until the meat is no longer pink, then stir through the sake or wine, the miso and the doubanjiang, followed by the stock. When it begins to simmer, turn the heat down to medium, add the tofu and cook for a further 1–2 minutes. Add the starchy slurry you prepared at the beginning and continue cooking until the sauce thickens nicely, it should take about 1 minute.

Serve immediately over the donburi bowls of rice, sprinkled with the reserved spring onion greens.

お

米

VEGETABLES

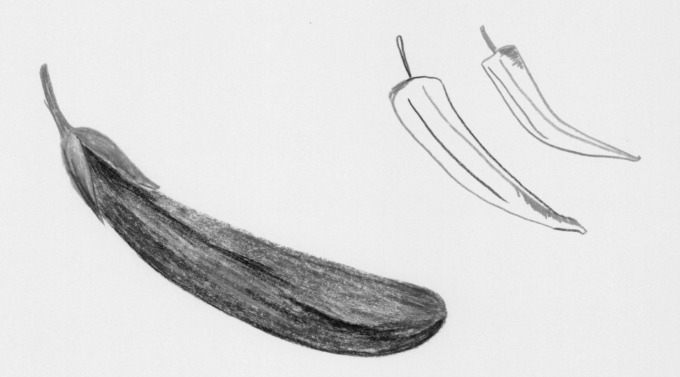

御

SHUN,
THE JOY OF
PEAK SEASONALITY

旬

Long before I moved to Italy, I learned about eating seasonally from our family's annual visits to my grandparents in Japan. Seasonality is an integral part of the Japanese psyche, a way of being. Our meals were always punctuated with hints at the season: the appearance of takenoko (freshly harvested bamboo shoots) after the snow melts in spring and juicy, fragrant strawberries; vegetables like cucumber, eggplant (aubergine) and reviving okra in the summer, along with refreshing flavours like shiso and myoga (Japanese ginger shoots) and the tastiest, ripest, blushing white peaches I have ever eaten; new rice, matsutake mushrooms, chestnuts and ginkgo nuts in autumn (fall); a windowsill full of picked persimmons waiting to ripen with the frost and my favourite vegetables in winter: daikon and lotus root.

Seasonality and a connection to nature is so important in Japanese culture that there are even special words and phrases with no direct English translation. *Kisetsukan* (季節感) is a phrase that describes having a 'sense of the seasons' or the 'feeling of seasonality', which you can use to describe a painting as much as the new seasonal offers at the market. And the word *hashiri* (走り) refers to the first harvest (or catch, if it is fish) of the season, a highly anticipated and much-appreciated find, whether on a sushi menu or at a market stall.

There is also the concept of *shun* (旬), which describes the joy of eating food at its very peak of seasonality, when a fruit or vegetable is at its perfect ripeness, or meat or fish are at their best, most flavourful moment. Shun was also important in ancient Japanese medicine: by eating a diet of shun ingredients, it was believed, you would have not only a healthy life but a happy, balanced one. We now know for certain that vegetables and fruits are significantly more nutritious when at their peak season and, well, it is hard to ignore that they are just simply more enjoyable to eat in season, too.

Even the tableware you choose should involve this sense of seasonality and will enhance how you feel as you eat. A plate with a cool blue hue in the midst of a sweltering summer will make you feel cooler, as will frosty glassware that looks like ice – my mother has a plate like this that she always serves sashimi on and it's as if she is bringing out a slab of ice. Spring foods might be served on brightly coloured plates to remind you of the blossoms in bloom, while autumn might bring more earthy tones and even a maple leaf here or there as a decoration on the side of a plate. ●

113

飯

PICKLES
AND SALADS

漬物とサラダ

Japanese pickles, or tsukemono, make up an important part of Japanese meals, used for their crunch and texture as well as their balancing sweet-and-sour flavour profile, which can act as a welcome palate cleanser. But deeper than that, pickles are also a constant marker of the season, a regular part of the calendar and a tradition that is passed down through families. London-based Japanese chef and teacher, Sachiko Saeki, puts it beautifully: 'In the making of miso and pickles lies process and alchemy, while fermenting seasonal vegetables puts me in a cyclical time. Pickling is a very special activity. What I am doing as a chef is also part of my family history, too. I often remember particular foods or dishes my parents, grandmother and auntie used to make.'

Tsukemono can be served in tiny bowls as a snack before a meal alongside sake; as a garnish to brighten a rich or heavy dish, such as Japanese curry or okonomiyaki; or simply served just with rice – a single umeboshi (pickled plum) in the centre of a bowl of rice is perhaps the ultimate pickle pairing, and reminiscent of the Japanese flag (they're called 'hinomaru bento' after the name of the national flag, when you see it in the form of a bento box).

Vegetables are usually pickled relatively quickly in salt, sugar, soy sauce, rice vinegar, rice bran or even koji (the cultured mould used to make miso, soy sauce and alcohol, such as sake and shochu – a spirit distilled with rice or other grains), and are enjoyed as part of an everyday meal.

Salads (you could call them aemono in Japanese, 'dressed things') are perhaps a more modern, Westernised addition to the Japanese table, and can often be treated like partially pickled vegetables too – thinly sliced, to add bite and freshness to the meal – or are made up of cooked vegetables, served cold and 'dressed' in sauces made of ground sesame and creamy tofu, miso, Japanese mayonnaise or simply rice vinegar. ●

114

御

SOME BELOVED
JAPANESE VEGETABLES

よく使われる日本の野菜

It probably is quite clear by now that Japanese cuisine is a vegetable-forward one, but what you may not know is that Japan is almost fully self-sustaining when it comes to producing vegetables. In a USDA foreign agricultural report from 2018, it was found that only 5 per cent of vegetables in Japan were imported, the rest are grown locally (if you are curious, that 5 per cent includes specific things like potatoes for chips, broccoli and celery). Like the pantry essentials, you won't have to go too far to find a few basics in the fridge to cook these dishes, although there are some that I want to highlight so you can keep your eye out for them, perhaps at your local Asian grocer. Or maybe you can even find some seeds for these heirlooms that you can plant. My parents have a collection of Japanese plants in pots that they keep in their courtyard, including mitsuba (Japanese wild chervil), shiso, sansho (Japanese pepper – the fragrant leaves, berries and pods are all used) and yuzu (Japanese citrus). It is such a treat to have these aromatics always fresh and on hand.

CABBAGE
KYABETSU キャベツ

Although not a traditional Japanese vegetable, it is one that suits Japanese cuisine so well and is a must for dishes such as tonkatsu and okonomiyaki. It became a staple after the Second World War and can be found grown year-round in Japan – you might be surprised to know that it is the second-largest vegetable crop in Japan after potatoes. Hakusai, which is Chinese cabbage or napa cabbage, is also common and often used for stews and pickles.

CHESTNUT
KURI 栗

The symbol of autumn (fall), chestnut is a much-appreciated ingredient in Japanese cooking for its sweet flavour and versatility in both sweet and savoury dishes. It is often cooked with rice for kuri gohan or is found in desserts like yokan (a red bean jelly). For the best results, use fresh, in-season chestnuts, but in a pinch already cooked and peeled chestnuts can be used.

CORN
TŌMOROKOSHI OR KON コーン

Japan has a great love of corn. You can find it in countless dishes. Another borrowed ingredient from the New World, corn initially was brought over by the Portuguese in the 16th century, but it was mostly used to feed working animals. Eventually, in the 1900s, sweetcorn was planted in Hokkaido and it has since made its way into the hearts and homes of many popular dishes in Japan from rice, to buns, to ramen and a childhood favourite, corn soup.

CUCUMBER
KYURI キュウリ

Cucumber is not native to Japan (its name written in katakana, the Japanese characters reserved for foreign words, gives this away) but, like corn, has become such an important part of the everyday

115

飯

cuisine – they are a must for pickles and salads. Originating in India, cucumber became popular in Japan in the 17th century. The Japanese varieties are extremely pleasingly crunchy with few seeds and no bitterness.

DAIKON
大根

For me, daikon (which literally means 'big root') is *the* most indispensable Japanese vegetable – its flavour and aroma are so representative of Japanese home cooking. Air-dried, freeze-dried, simmered, pickled, grated, rehydrated, this giant white radish can be prepared in so many ways you would need an entire cookbook alone to describe them all. It's like the tomato is to Italian cooking. Raw daikon is much appreciated as a foil to fried foods and is said to aid digestion, so you will often see a mound of perfectly white, fluffy, finely grated daikon accompanying dishes where you might need some help.

EGGPLANT (AUBERGINE)
NASU / なす

One of the most popular vegetables in Japan, there are a number of different varieties of Japanese eggplant, some of which are petite, baby versions, or long and thin with sweet, bright white flesh. They are a symbol of summer eating and are used in fried dishes like tempura or Miso eggplant (page 200), turned into pickles or boiled in miso soup and more. Like cucumbers, Japanese eggplants do not have the bitterness of their Western counterparts, so there is not a tradition of salting them before cooking. Eggplants are a symbol of good luck in Japan, especially if you dream of one in the new year – the word nasu sounds similar to the word 'to accomplish'. To give you one final insight into this beloved vegetable, I want to share with you this phrase: 'Don't let your daughter-in-law eat your autumn (fall) eggplants' (*akinasu wa yome ni kuwasuna* / 秋茄子は嫁に食わすな), meaning don't let yourself get taken advantage of; used to describe

something so delicious that a mother-in-law wouldn't even share it with her daughter-in-law, because those autumn eggplants are the best of all.

GINGER
SHOGA しょうが

There are two types of Japanese ginger, the rhizome or the root is one you are probably already familiar with, while the pink shoot or bud – myoga (みょうが) – is incredibly fragrant and used as an aromatic garnish for sashimi or noodles and is harder to come across outside of Japan (but easy to grow!). Fresh, finely grated ginger is an uplifting, invigorating addition to the top of many dishes from soba noodles to fresh, chilled tofu (page 50), while gari (young pickled ginger, page 35) is a must with sashimi and sushi, and the stronger red pickles known as Beni shoga (page 36) are indispensable on street food dishes like yakisoba, takoyaki and okonomiyaki.

KABOCHA
かぼちゃ

This small, dark-skinned pumpkin or squash is an incredibly sweet, floury pumpkin that tastes like chestnuts. It is delicious simmered as Nimono (page 138) or fried in tempura, and as it is so sweet, is even popular in seasonal desserts and buns, in a version of Anpan (page 235). The skin is so thin and soft you can – and should – eat it. As important as kabocha is in Japanese kitchens, it is native to Central America and was brought to Japan in the 16th century by the Portuguese via Cambodia.

LOTUS ROOT
RENKON / 蓮根

The rhizome (though mistakenly referred to as a root) of the lotus flower, is a delicious, crisp vegetable, much-loved in Japanese home cooking. You can simmer, fry or braise it in numerous dishes and it is also delicious sandwiching a meat filling and fried for the New Year meal, Osechi Ryori. It also has quite a special place in Japanese Buddhism, because the lotus, a beautiful flower that grows from murky waters, is a symbol of reincarnation or attaining enlightenment.

OKRA
OKURA / オクラ

Although not originally from Japan (it likely came from its native Ethiopia to the Americas during the slave trade in the 16th century, then from America to Japan in the 19th century after the country opened up from its self-imposed isolation), this is a vegetable that is well appreciated in Japanese cuisine for its 'neba neba' consistency when cooked – in other words, slimy. Even the flowers, which look like beautiful, pale yellow hibiscus flowers, are used in cooking, often simply chopped and added to dishes as a garnish. It is very nutritious and has many health benefits, but is particularly loved as a refreshing vegetable to enjoy in the summer.

SHISO
紫蘇

Also known as perilla, or Japanese mint (it is part of the mint family after all), this intensely fragrant leaf comes in two kinds: red and green. The red, akashiso, is what lends its deep colouring to umeboshi (pickled plums) (and in turn to beni shoga, which is ginger pickled in the juices lef over from making umeboshi), while regular green shiso is used to garnish and flavour fresh dishes like sashimi and Chilled tofu (page 50). It's delicious fried like tempura (you can even fry the buds when the plant has gone to seed) and makes a perfumed, pretty (edible) divider in bento boxes.

SPRING ONION (SCALLION)
NEGI / ネギ OR ねぎ

Also known as welsh onion, this is a stalwart of Japanese cooking. Brought to Japan from its native China in the Nara period of the 8th century, you can find it in almost every traditional dish. It's not quite a leek and not quite the same as the common spring onions you may find (although this is what I call for throughout the book, because real Japanese negi, *Allium fistulosum*, is hard to get outside of Japan). Negi is thicker and can withstand quite lengthy cooking. Both the white and green parts are used in cooking, in different ways. They can be cooked in dishes like yakitori and Sukiyaki (page 177), where their flavour becomes intensely sweet, or used as a spicy, fresh, raw garnish (especially the green parts, to add colour). The best time for negi is between December and February.

TARO
SATOIMO / 里芋

Japanese taro, a little smaller than its taro relatives found elsewhere, are a little like hairy potatoes, but with a creamy, slightly sticky texture that soaks up flavours well. They are most often simmered in stews or in soups. These unassuming little root vegetables happen to be highly nutritious, full of fibre, excellent for balancing blood sugar and for gut health. Some people are sensitive to the calcium oxalate found in raw taro (like some other popular Japanese root vegetables, such as mountain yams) – it can cause itchiness on the skin when handled raw but this effect will disappear once cooked. ●

117

Daikon and Carrot Salad

SERVES 4 AS A SIDE DISH

紅
白
な
ま
す

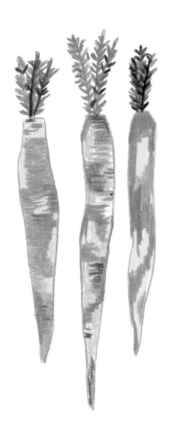

118

Namasu refers to a dish of raw vegetables lightly marinated in sweetened vinegar, and this particular colourful winter side dish is the best-known. Although it can (and should) be enjoyed any time you can find good daikon, it is always a part of auspicious New Year celebrations, or Osechi Ryori, where the orange of the carrots and the bright white of the daikon mimic the traditional celebratory colours of red and white. Red Japanese carrots, known as kintoki ninjin, with their distinctly deep colour and sweet flavour, can be enjoyed at their shun peak in December and January, making them highly sought-after in a perfect New Year's Eve meal.

The flavour of this dressing should be a delicate balance between sweet and mildly acidic, which is why rice vinegar (not other types of vinegar) is vital here. If you are lucky enough to have fresh yuzu, you can add some of the zest or juice, even a splash of bottled yuzu juice, for an extra-special touch.

METHOD

Peel and cut the vegetables into matchsticks, then place them in a bowl with a good, three-fingered pinch of salt. Toss the salt with the vegetables really well, then leave to rest for 5–10 minutes.

Meanwhile, prepare the dressing by mixing the rice vinegar and sugar with another pinch of salt, remembering that the vegetables are already a little salted. They should have released some liquid now, so drain them of their salt water, rinse briefly with fresh water and gently squeeze out any excess liquid. Pat dry on a clean dish towel and toss them in the dressing.

This can be enjoyed immediately, or you can even prepare this dish a few days in advance. Keep it in an airtight container in the fridge until needed.

INGREDIENTS

1 carrot
12–15 cm (4¾–6 in) piece of daikon
salt
2 tablespoons rice vinegar
2 teaspoons sugar

御

Cucumber and Sesame Salad

SERVES 4 AS A SIDE DISH

きゅうりとゴマのサラダ

119

If you haven't tasted cucumbers in Japan before, then you won't have realised exactly what an incredibly delicious vegetable this can be. Japanese cucumbers are unlike any other I have ever tasted – impossibly crunchy, sweet and thin, with an often extremely prickly skin and barely any seeds. When I get a chance to eat them in Japan, I get my fill. I love them served chilled in the summer with a dipping sauce of sweet miso – one of the best snacks in the world – or accompanying wakame in the classic salad that you might find in Japanese restaurants all over the world. But this recipe, a very simple salad of slightly 'wilted' cucumber slices (they soak up the flavours better this way) and a sweet-salty dressing with earthy sesame oil and warmth from a touch of shichimi togarashi, is one that I love to make at home to go with anything, even a bowl of rice.

INGREDIENTS

1 thin, firm, long cucumber (see note)
a pinch of salt
2 teaspoons soy sauce
2 teaspoons sesame oil
1 tablespoon toasted, ground sesame
   seeds (see note)
a pinch of sugar
a pinch of shichimi togarashi or chilli
   powder (optional)

NOTE

Go for a firm, fresh cucumber, such as Japanese or Lebanese varieties, for a salad like this, you won't need to peel it if it is a good one. If it is older or thicker, you may find it has too many watery seeds or the skin is quite bitter. These aren't the right kind of cucumbers for this dish. If you grind the toasted sesame seeds in a suribachi (or a mortar and pestle) you get this rough 'powder' of sesame, which is absolutely delicious. If you don't have any way to do this, just sprinkle over whole toasted sesame seeds.

METHOD

Thinly slice the cucumber (no need to peel if it is a good one). Add a good pinch of salt and massage it through the slices, then let it rest while you prepare the dressing.

Combine the remaining ingredients together and mix until the sugar is dissolved.

The cucumbers should have released some water by now because of the salt. Drain, give them a quick rinse in fresh water, gently squeeze out any excess water, then pat dry with a clean dish towel. Place in a bowl with the dressing and serve.

飯

Fried and Braised Lotus Root and Carrot

SERVES 4 AS A SIDE DISH

蓮根のきんぴら

I could eat an entire panful of Obaachan's kinpira to myself, and have often done just that. It is a humble, simple dish, but it is the one I think of first when I think of my favourite dishes of hers. Sometimes this is made with gobo (burdock root), sometimes just with lotus root, but I love this combination – the crunch and stickiness of the lotus, the sweetness of the carrot. My mother adds fresh slices of hot red chilli, too, which is an excellent idea.

120

INGREDIENTS

300 g (10½ oz) lotus root, thinly sliced (see note)
1 tablespoon sake
1 tablespoon mirin
1 teaspoon sugar
1 tablespoon sesame oil
1 large carrot, peeled and thinly sliced on the diagonal
1 tablespoon soy sauce

NOTE

If you find it difficult to find fresh lotus root, you can look for pre-cut, frozen lotus root at Asian grocers. I find these are often too thick for this dish. Although it's a bit fiddly, you can defrost the thick slices and then carefully slice them as thinly as you can to use here.

METHOD

Soak the slices of lotus root in some cold water for 5 minutes to avoid discolouration (some like to add a splash of rice vinegar to this mixture), then pat dry.

Meanwhile, combine the sake, mirin and sugar and stir to dissolve the sugar.

Heat a frying pan (skillet) over a medium–high heat, add the sesame oil and begin frying the lotus root and carrot slices, tossing frequently with a spatula (or chopsticks) to ensure even cooking. After about 5 minutes, when the vegetables are about halfway cooked, add the sake mixture and continue cooking until the liquid is almost entirely evaporated and the vegetables are just about done, at most a further 5 minutes. The lotus root should still have some crunch to it, the carrots should be sweet and a little soft and both should have some lovely browning (but not too much so be careful, as the sugars in both lotus root and carrot tend to make them brown very easily). Add the soy sauce, toss quickly to coat the vegetables and remove from the heat.

Serve hot, tepid, or even cold the next day.

御

飯

御

Spring Onions in Miso-Vinegar Dressing

SERVES 4 AS A SMALL SIDE DISH

ネ
ギ
ぬ
た

Nuta is an old-fashioned but incredibly delicious dish featuring a miso-vinegar sauce that my grandmother used to make often with poached squid and spring onions. It is usually made with seafood – you could add cooked clams or raw tuna sashimi, for example – but the spring onion is non-negotiable here (well, technically, negi is the slightly thicker welsh onion – if you can find it, it is a little heartier and sturdier than regular spring onions). In fact, as a vegetarian version (minus the shellfish), I love the idea of the spring onions here as the star, so often just a background note or a garnish. It makes a wonderful little dish as an appetiser to go with sake while waiting for a main meal, or add several other small vegetable side dishes, some rice and miso soup and you have a full meal. If you like a little heat, a tiny bit of Japanese mustard or hot English mustard goes well here too.

123

METHOD

Ensure the clams are purged before starting. Steam them open in a lidded pan over a high heat with a splash of sake or water; it should take 1–2 minutes for them all to open. Set aside.

Mix the miso, sugar and rice vinegar together until smooth. Add a splash of water to loosen the sauce a little, if necessary. Place in a small saucepan and warm gently, just until the sugar dissolves. Set aside.

Bring a small pan of water to the boil and blanch the spring onions until they wilt, about 1 minute. Drain and plunge into a bowl of cool water, then drain again well before mixing with the miso-vinegar sauce and the clams. This is good warm or cold.

INGREDIENTS

250 g (9 oz) live clams, such as vongole veraci, rinsed and purged (see page 57)
a splash of sake (optional)
2 tablespoons white or brown miso
1 tablespoon sugar
1 tablespoon rice vinegar
1 bunch of spring onions (scallions), roots trimmed, green and white parts cut into 3 cm (1¼ in) sections

飯

Mushrooms with Tofu, Miso and Sesame Dressing

SERVES 4 AS A SIDE DISH

きのこの白和え

If you thought tofu dishes were bland, you haven't tried Japanese dishes like shiraae. This is a thick and luscious sauce made with tofu, miso and sesame paste or ground sesame seeds that is delicious with any seasonal, blanched vegetables. The sauce is so good I have been known to just eat it out of the bowl with a spoon. I love this preparation with any vegetables, especially green beans, broccoli, asparagus or spinach, for example spinach (if using spinach, double the amount indicated in the ingredients). But you don't have to stick to greens, this really goes well with anything – mushrooms or carrots, too! I've used pioppini or honey fungus mushrooms here, which are a little similar to shimeji mushrooms.

124

INGREDIENTS

200 g (7 oz) vegetables of your choice (see introduction)
a drizzle of vegetable oil (optional)
salt (optional)

SHIRAAE SAUCE
120 g (4½ oz) silken tofu
1 tablespoon ground toasted sesame seeds (or sesame paste), plus extra to serve
1 teaspoon sugar
1 teaspoon soy sauce
1 teaspoon white miso

METHOD

The first thing to do is drain and 'press' the tofu. Carefully remove the silken tofu from its packet and place it on a plate. Pop another plate on top and a light weight (unless the plate itself is heavy enough) and leave for 15 minutes. During this time, some excess liquid should seep out. Drain and pat dry with kitchen paper.

Place the tofu in a suribachi (or mortar and pestle) and add the ground sesame seeds, sugar, soy sauce and miso. Grind until you have a smooth, thick paste.

Next, prepare your chosen vegetable. If using mushrooms, simply pan fry them in a drizzle of vegetable oil until just cooked, about 2 minutes. If using greens, blanch in salted boiling water until just cooked, 1–2 minutes at most (be careful not to overcook), then drain, plunge into some ice-cold water, drain well and pat dry.

Toss the cooked veg with the shiraae sauce and add an extra sprinkle of ground sesame seeds, if you like.

御

Shiraae is one of the many preparations that have come from shojin ryori, the simple, vegetarian cuisine of Zen Buddhism, which is centred around tofu and seasonal vegetables. Others include tempura, namasu and natto. There are special considerations with shojin ryori, not only avoiding any meat or seafood products, but even abstaining from alcohol (so no mirin or sake in the cooking) or strong flavours like garlic and onion (too exciting) – all of these things interfered with meditation. However, the style of cuisine is far from bland and shiraae is a wonderful example. Attention is paid to ensure the five colours – red, white, black, green and yellow – and the five flavours – bitter, sweet, sour, salty and umami – are present in every meal. There is also an ancient no-waste philosophy of 'eating the whole', where leafy daikon tops and vegetable peels might be re-used in other dishes – perhaps the soup that forms part of the ichi ju san sai meal (one soup and three dishes – rice is always included in this, too).

125

飯

Seasoned Okra

SERVES 4 AS A SIDE DISH

オ
ク
ラ
の
お
ひ
た
し

You can make this with spinach, green beans or asparagus if okra is not your thing, but if it is, read on, because this wonderful, nutritious vegetable (actually it is technically a fruit) is much-loved in Japan and this is considered an excellent, cool summertime dish precisely because of the thing that causes many people to shy away from it: its sticky 'mucilage'. Like natto, this stringy, slimy texture is a much-appreciated quality in Japanese cuisine, and it is also what makes this very good for your digestion. Boiling okra for too long enhances the stickiness, so you can boil this for anywhere between 2 and 10 minutes, depending on your preference. The lemon juice isn't traditional here, it's normally simply dressed with soy sauce and katsuobushi, but with the okra it is a really lovely, fresh addition.

126

INGREDIENTS

250 g (9 oz) okra (about 20)
2 teaspoons soy sauce
2 teaspoons lemon juice (optional)
1–2 big pinches of katsuobushi
   (dried bonito flakes)

METHOD

Boil the okra as you like (I go for 2–3 minutes). Drain and plunge into a bowl of ice-cold water to stop the cooking process. Drain again.

Remove and discard the top stems of the okra and cut the rest into 5 mm (¼ in) rounds (very pretty as they look like stars), then toss with the soy sauce and lemon juice, if using. Distribute among serving dishes and top each dish with some katsuobushi.

御

飯

御

Like the shiraae (page 124), this is one of my favourite easy dressings to put on any vegetable that was often on my obaachan's table – try this with blanched broccoli, spinach, snow peas (mangetout), or even grated carrot is delicious with this sesame dressing.

If you are starting with raw sesame seeds (which are white rather than golden brown), toasting them brings out their best, nuttiest flavour. Place the sesame seeds in a small dry frying pan (in Japan they have a special pan for this known as a goma iriki, with an attached wire mesh lid to protect the seeds from popping out of the pan – they can jump like popcorn). To do this without a lid, you just need to be careful and quick, because sesame seeds can burn quickly. Place over a low heat and swirl or toss the seeds gently as they heat up. They should turn hazelnut brown within about 2–3 minutes, but do not go much darker than that. Remove them instantly to a jar or a small bowl – if you leave them in the pan, they continue cooking and popping!

The sugar in the recipe is to counter the slight bitterness of the sesame paste and the saltiness of the soy sauce; if using tahini or another kind of sesame paste, go by taste, adding just a little at a time until the dressing is irresistible – it's all about balance.

Green Beans with Sesame Dressing

SERVES 4 AS A SMALL SIDE DISH

いんげんの胡麻和え

129

METHOD

Combine the dressing ingredients along with 1–2 tablespoons of water to help loosen it until you have a smooth sauce.

Blanch the green beans in boiling salted water for 1–2 minutes. Drain, then plunge into ice-cold water to stop the cooking. Drain again.

Mix the beans with 1–2 tablespoons of the dressing until evenly coated, then serve with an extra sprinkling of toasted sesame seeds.

INGREDIENTS
200 g (7 oz) green beans
salt

SESAME DRESSING
1 tablespoon sesame paste
1 tablespoon toasted ground
 sesame seeds, plus extra to serve
1 teaspoon sugar, or to taste
2 teaspoons soy sauce

飯

Okara Salad

SERVES 4–6 AS A SIDE DISH

おから
サラダ

130

Okara is the by-product of tofu-making. Yellow soybeans are blended with spring water to create a smoothie-like puree – the puree is then strained, giving you soy milk with which to make tofu, and a dry, pulpy mass – in other words, okara. It is very cheap to purchase in Japan, but also easy to make at home and especially useful if you like to drink fresh soy milk or make your own tofu (page 47). While okara doesn't have much flavour itself, it is excellent at soaking up flavours (which it does well in this dish) and it is incredibly nutritious, so it is worth experimenting with – it can add bulk to hamburgers or home-made bread and I've even had it in delicious doughnuts topped with kuromitsu (black sugar syrup) in Nagano. But this salad is probably my favourite, maybe because it tastes like my obaachan's cooking and when I eat this I am right back on a wooden bench at her table.

This is a combination of vegetables and colours that I like, but you can feel free to use what you have on hand or what is in season: asparagus, snow peas (mangetout), mung bean sprouts, spring onions (scallions), lotus root or other Japanese mushrooms like enoki could all go in here. Hijiki seaweed is hard to weigh as it is so light and it is hard to measure as it is often sold in a tangle of dried, pre-cooked strands, so don't get too hung up about the measurements here for this salad – I've said a big pinch because you'll find it expands enormously when it rehydrates, and if you want more, you can simply add more.

METHOD

It is a good idea to fry the okara in a dry pan (that has a lid) if it is quite damp like wet sand. Doing this just removes some of the excess moisture. Cook for 2–3 minutes over a medium heat, or until it has lost some moisture. Set aside.

Place the hijiki seaweed in some water to rehydrate for about 10 minutes.

Place the mushrooms in a small bowl, cover with hot water and let steep for 20 minutes. When rehydrated, slice off and discard the stems, and cut the rest into thin slices. Filter the soaking water through a tea strainer and set aside.

Drizzle the vegetable oil into the same pan that you used for the okara earlier. Stir-fry the carrot and mushrooms for 1 minute over a medium–high heat, then add about 80 ml ($^1/_3$ cup) of the reserved shiitake stock along with the soy sauce, mirin and salt. Cover immediately with the pan lid and cook for 2–3 minutes, then add the okara and cook, tossing, for a few more minutes or until the liquid reduces slightly. Add the green beans and continue tossing until the beans are cooked but still have some crunch and bright colour, about 2 minutes, then stir in the hijiki (as it is pre-cooked it doesn't need to cook).

Remove from the heat and enjoy. This is delicious cold, too, but do take note that okara doesn't last very long, so eat this as fresh as possible. At most, you can keep it for 1–2 days in the fridge.

INGREDIENTS

180 g (1 cup) okara
a large pinch of dried hijiki seaweed
3 dried shiitake mushrooms
a drizzle of vegetable oil
½ carrot, peeled and cut into matchsticks
2 tablespoons soy sauce
1 tablespoon mirin
¼ teaspoon salt
50 g (1¾ oz) (about a handful) of green beans, sliced thinly on the diagonal

御

飯

Cabbage Salad with Daikon Citrus Dressing

SERVES 4 AS A SIDE DISH

キャベツの千切りサラダ

132

This is one of my favourite salads, refreshing, crunchy, with a welcome little zing of citrus (yuzu if you have it, otherwise lemon), which is rather reminiscent of ponzu sauce. This type of fine shredding, like the traditional accompaniment for tonkatsu, is called sengiri (千切り) and means 'a thousand cuts'. Daikon is often added to fried dishes to help improve digestion and cleanse the palate, so its presence in this salad makes it the perfect accompaniment to anything fried or even richer dishes, such as the Sweet soy baked chicken wings (page 198), Grilled fish (page 59) or Miso eggplant (page 200).

In Japan, you can buy special graters for vegetables such as daikon and ginger, called oroshigane (下ろし金) or oroshiki (下ろし器), which grate the vegetables quickly into a really fine paste. My favourite one for doing this job is a ceramic plate with a rough centre of fine spikes, but often they are made out of metal or even wood. If you don't have one, the smallest holes on a box grater or a microplane will do, though it won't be as fine.

INGREDIENTS

¼ head of cabbage, finely shredded
5 cm (2 in) piece of daikon, finely grated
1 tablespoon soy sauce
juice of 1 lemon or yuzu
1 tablespoon sesame oil
½ teaspoon sugar
2 teaspoons toasted sesame seeds

METHOD

Place the shredded cabbage in a serving bowl.

Combine the remaining ingredients and pour evenly over the cabbage. Serve immediately.

御

飯

御

Smoky Eggplants

SERVES 4 AS A SIDE DISH

焼
き
な
す

Eggplants (aubergines) are a much-loved late-summer vegetable in Japan; they feature heavily in seasonal cooking, from soups, pickles, tempura, with miso (a favourite, page 200), braised and more. There are a number of different varieties of Japanese eggplant, some of which are petite, baby versions (konasu, 小なす) or thin and long, with creamy, sweet, bright-white flesh – and these are what you need (size-wise) for this dish in order for this cooking technique to work rather than a large, more common globe eggplant.

You do need some kind of open flame for this dish, like a barbecue or even an open fireplace or a camp fire! My mother often makes this dish in the summer and I love how quickly and simply it comes together. With a hint of smokiness coming through, all you need is a splash of soy sauce, and one simple garnish: I love it with katsuobushi, but thinly sliced spring onions (scallions), toasted sesame seeds or some finely grated fresh ginger are all delicious options.

135

METHOD

Rinse and pat dry the whole eggplants. Place them directly over a flame, such as on a barbecue or directly on the gas hob if you have a gas stove top. Turn regularly until the skin is completely and evenly blackened, about 10 minutes in total. Leave to cool completely, then carefully peel away the skin.

Serve with the soy sauce drizzled over the top and a sprinkle of katsuobushi or your garnish of choice.

INGREDIENTS

12 small baby eggplants (aubergines)
1 tablespoon soy sauce
a pinch of katsuobushi (dried bonito flakes) or see the introduction for other options

飯

Braised Eggplant

SERVES 4 AS A SIDE DISH

茄子の煮びたし

A classic of Japanese home cooking, this simple but elegant-looking dish of eggplant (aubergine) braised in dashi flavoured with ginger and soy sauce is so much more than the sum of its parts. As the eggplant sits in the braising liquid to cool it absorbs so much flavour. It's a nice dish to make ahead of time for this reason, and it's also just as delicious cold as it is warm. The long, thin eggplants I mentioned on page 135 are perfect for this dish.

METHOD

The eggplants should first be cut into sections about 7.5 cm (3 in) long, halved lengthways and scored on the skin sides with a sharp knife.

In a well-greased, deep pan, brown the eggplant over a medium–high heat on both sides to get some colour on them, about 3–4 minutes. Add the dashi, sake, soy sauce, mirin, sugar and half of the ginger, then reduce the heat to low–medium and bring to a simmer. Place a lid over the top (or a drop lid, fashioned out of a round of baking paper if you don't have one) and braise until the eggplants are very tender, about 10–15 minutes. Leave to cool in the sauce, which is where all the magic happens.

Serve sprinkled with the spring onion and the rest of the grated ginger on top.

INGREDIENTS
2 long Japanese eggplants (aubergines)
vegetable oil for greasing
250 ml (1 cup) Dashi (page 30)
2 tablespoons sake
2 tablespoons soy sauce
1 tablespoon mirin
1 tablespoon sugar
1 tablespoon finely grated root ginger
1 spring onion (scallion), finely chopped

御

飯

Braised Tofu

SERVES 4

This warming, comforting dish came about one day as I had both leftover sukiyaki sauce and some very fresh tofu and it must be one of the tastiest ways to enjoy tofu – I not-so-secretly love picking out the tofu from the sukiyaki pot. I only had spring onions to add to it (also a favourite element to fish out of the sukiyaki) and I kept thinking you could flesh this out into a bigger dish – by adding a soft-boiled egg, perhaps, or some mushrooms, spinach or bok choy (pak choy). As I ate it, I thought it reminded me of another wonderfully homely dish called nikudofu, where thin strips of beef are braised with the tofu in a similar sauce. But since making it again and again, I really prefer this way whenever I have a craving for sukiyaki but just want to keep things very simple.

138

INGREDIENTS

320 g (11½ oz) firm tofu, cut into thick slices
½ onion, sliced
2 spring onions (scallions) or ½ leek, cut into 1–2 cm (½–¾ in) diagonal slices
Steamed rice (page 80) and your favourite vegetable sides, to serve (optional)

SAUCE
60 ml (¼ cup) soy sauce
60 ml (¼ cup) mirin
60 ml (¼ cup) sake
2 teaspoons sugar
180 ml (¾ cup) water

METHOD

Bring the sauce ingredients to a simmer in a small-medium saucepan. Gently add the tofu and onion (make sure all the tofu is submerged under the precious liquid; if not, top up with some water until it is) and continue simmering, covered with a lid (or a drop lid, fashioned out of a round of baking paper) for 7–10 minutes, or until the onion is sweet and soft. Add the spring onions and cook for a further 3 minutes, or until it has given way and is wilted and tender (if using leek, it will need cooking for longer).

Serve with freshly steamed rice and two or three of the other vegetable side dishes in this chapter for a filling, satisfying vegetarian meal.

御

飯

Pumpkin Braised in Milk

SERVES 4 AS A SIDE DISH

かぼちゃのミルク煮

140

Soy sauce–spiked milk turns into the most delicious, soft curds in this silky sweet pumpkin dish, which seems an unlikely combination considering that milk has not long been a widespread part of Japanese cuisine.

In fact, until the 19th century, milk, like red meat, was taboo. Actually, milk and dairy products have been around since about the 7th century, but it wasn't until the Meiji era, when the ban on animal products was officially lifted, that they began to flourish. By the 1950s, in a postwar recovery effort, milk became a part of the national school lunch program, which helped it become an everyday food. Today, the place that is synonymous with fresh milk in Japan is Hokkaido, in the far north of the country, which has a climate and land more suitable for dairy farming than the humid, rugged and mountainous regions further south. It's interesting to note that there are two ways to say milk in Japanese, one is written in kanji characters: gyunyu 牛乳, while the other is an adaption of the English word, miruku, and so it is written in katakana, the set of characters used only for foreign words: ミルク. The difference is that gyunyu is simply whole milk and miruku usually describes a milk product.

So, this is a rather unusual dish, but it is so delicious. The small, dark green–skinned kabocha (also known as Japanese pumpkin or squash) with bright orange flesh is best for this recipe because it is wonderfully sweet and nutty with a floury consistency that reminds me of chestnuts. As it cooks, the edges soften and become incorporated into the creamy dressing. You could use butternut pumpkin (squash) or sweet potato as a substitute, but another reason I love Japanese pumpkin is that you can (and should) eat the skin. I have found the prized Italian pumpkin zucca mantovana is practically identical to a proper kabocha.

Like most simmered dishes in Japanese cuisine, gentle cooking is key, so that the pumpkin does not get mushy. But if you do go too far, have no fear: add a splash of rice wine vinegar and eat it cold the next day. It's a rather welcome substitute to creamy potato salad, and I have to admit perhaps my favourite way to have it. This would be ideal in a lunchtime bento box or as a side dish to some grilled fish or meat.

METHOD

Chop the pumpkin into small chunks, about 2.5 cm (1 in) long. Remove the seeds but leave the skin on, which not only adds flavour and creates a nice contrast in colour and texture, but it also will help the pumpkin retain its shape.

In a small saucepan, combine all the ingredients except for the vinegar. Bring to a simmer and cook gently over a low heat, uncovered, for 10 minutes, then cover with a lid until the pumpkin is soft but not falling apart and the milk has turned into thick, creamy curds, faintly resembling ricotta, about 10 minutes.

Serve warm or cold with a splash of rice wine vinegar stirred through, if desired.

INGREDIENTS

400 g (14 oz) kabocha pumpkin, skin on
180 ml (¾ cup) milk
1 tablespoon soy sauce
2 teaspoons sugar
2 teaspoons rice wine vinegar
  (or to taste, if desired)

御

飯

御

Golden Taro and Potatoes in Soy Butter

SERVES 4 AS A SIDE DISH

バター醤油焼き
里芋とジャガイモの

Taro, a hairy little root vegetable, might not be on your radar if you're not already familiar with a lot of Asian or African cuisine, but if you can seek them out, this is such a delicious way to enjoy them. Satoimo (里芋), Japanese taro, can be cooked similarly to potatoes, often simmered in stews or in soups or served simply steamed or simmered in their skins and served peeled with salt or soy sauce, a dish known as kinukatsugi. They are starchy with a very creamy, almost glutinous (delightful) texture that soaks up flavours well, and – bonus – they happen to be highly nutritious, full of fibre and excellent for gut health. If you like, add a little garnish of some chopped spring onion or some warmth from shichimi togarashi or fresh chilli.

143

METHOD

Rinse the taro and scrub with a brush to remove some of the extra hairs, then (with gloves if you wish) peel with a sharp knife and cut into quarters or chunks of similar size. Peel the potatoes and cut into a similar size as the taro.

Place the vegetables in a pot of cold water and bring to the boil. Cook until a skewer or a fork goes in easily, about 10 minutes. You could also leave them this way and just toss the warm, boiled vegetables with the butter and soy sauce, or continue on to the next step if you would like the golden, crisp-on-the-outside version.

Heat a cast-iron pan over high heat and add the vegetable oil. Toss the vegetables in the oil to coat completely and then let them get golden brown and crisped on the outside, about 5–7 minutes.

Transfer to a bowl and add the butter (which should melt with the heat of the vegetables) and soy sauce, and toss to coat completely.

Serve immediately, with one or two of the suggested garnishes, if you like.

INGREDIENTS

4 Japanese taro
4 small new potatoes
1 tablespoon vegetable oil
2 tablespoons butter
2 tablespoons soy sauce

GARNISH
finely chopped spring onion (scallion),
 shichimi togarashi or finely sliced
 fresh chilli (optional)

NOTE

Some people are sensitive to the calcium oxalate that gives this vegetable a slightly slimy feel when raw, like some other popular Japanese root vegetables such as mountain yams. It can cause itchiness on the skin when handling raw but will disappear once cooked. I don't have a problem with satoimo as I do with the yams, but you can wear gloves to protect your hands just to be sure. You may also find ready-peeled, frozen taro in your local Asian grocer to avoid this problem, too.

飯

KONAMONO TO SUTORITO FUDO

フ　粉
ー　物
ド　と
　　ス
　　ト
　　リ
　　ー
　　ト
　　・

NOODLES & STREET FOOD

There is a term from the Kansai region for many of the dishes in this chapter, konamon or konamono, which means 'flour foods'. A concept that is less than a century old, this term developed to talk of foods that rely on flour, such as takoyaki (octopus balls) and okonomiyaki, which come from the Kansai region (in the south of Honshu, around Kyoto and Osaka), but it really encompasses any other staple food that isn't rice, especially wheat, but also buckwheat, which were grown in parts of Japan where the weather or the landscape was too extreme for rice crops, such as Aomori prefecture in northern Japan. Reliance on these foods in certain parts of Japan became especially important when rice wasn't plentiful or accessible. As Yukihiro Kasai, owner of his family's takoyaki business in Osaka writes, 'In times of war or famine, the konamons were affordable and satisfied the appetites.'

What I find so interesting is the division of starchy staples in Japan into two groups: rice or everything else, konamon – and that with konamon a very important culture of comforting dishes made with these staples grew. If soba is Tokyo's soul food, then okonomiyaki is Osaka's.

It is perhaps telling that I chose to call this book *Gohan* – 'rice'. I am a rice girl through and through. I was brought up on it (although perhaps in Australia in the early 1980s it was easier to get rice rather than udon or soba). But I adore Japanese noodles and in this chapter you can find the simple, versatile noodle dishes I love most of all and use as versatile building blocks. You will also find my favourite street foods turned family food – these are dishes that I loved as a child and that we often ate at home or on visits to Japan. They really have an irresistibly tasty, fun quality that wins everyone over. ●

THE ZEN BUDDHIST HISTORY OF NOODLES IN JAPAN

日本における禅宗の歴史と麺類の普及

While not as ancient as rice, noodles have a long history, with their beginnings in Buddhist monastery kitchens. They first date to the 8th century, when wheat was introduced to Japan from China through Zen Buddhist priests, as the story goes.

Hiroshi Ito, the owner of Nagaura, a soba restaurant in Ginza, where the specialty is an ancient style of Zen soba called terakata, wrote quite thoroughly about the Zen Buddhist roots of noodles, with much of his work involving delving into ancient accounts (including a 'secret soba' book). He describes the accounts of two medieval Zen priests who had studied extensively in Zhejiang province in China, thirty-five years apart, before bringing back their learnings to Japan, noting the use of flour noodles as a snack after back-breaking work for monks (rice, being a staple, was only allowed for meals), how to prepare and eat them, details of the Zen diet such as seasonings (the essential five flavours) and also the first accounts of powdered green tea. It transformed Zen Buddhist food in Japan and monastery kitchens became the place where noodle-making was developed and refined. Over the centuries, in Zen accounts, there are traces of the names of the noodles we know today: somen is one of the earliest mentioned, in 1340, then udon (spelled 'uton' at the time) in 1347, and finally soba is mentioned for the first time in a diary entry from 1438: 'Received a box of matsutake mushrooms and a box of soba from Shokoku-ji Temple's Rokuon-in Temple.'

Somen (very thin wheat noodles) probably had its origins as early as the Nara period (8th century) but in the form of rice noodles from China. Later, in the medieval Heian and Kamabura periods, there are accounts of thin noodles being made with wheat. These silky smooth, thin noodles, reminiscent of Italian angel hair pasta but thinner, were eaten at religious ceremonies for the Tanabata Festival on July 7 – it was believed that eating these silky, thin noodles for the festival would ward off serious illness.

Udon (thick, chewy wheat noodles) are famous in the area around Takamatsu in Kagawa prefecture on Shikoku island, where Takinomiya Temmangu

147

物

shrine lays claim to the medieval birthplace of udon. Not coincidentally, it's a place that was picked out centuries ago for having a favourable climate suitable for wheat farming. In their book *Japanese Soul Cooking*, Tadashi Ono and Harris Salat praise the square-cut sanuki udon from this area too and paint this picture of it today: 'Hundreds of udon joints dot this diminutive burg; "udon taxis", complete with huge plastic replicas of udon bowls lashed to their roofs, ferry passengers from shop to shop; and the city hosts a huge udon festival every year where... noodles are consecrated at local temples.' The udon enthusiast's dream.

Soba has a similarly long and special history, in particular in Tokyo. While buckwheat itself has been around since ancient times, buckwheat noodles as we know them today did not make their debut until the 16th century. Prior to that, buckwheat was cooked like a polenta or into thick dumplings or rice cakes. Zen Buddhist monks would eat these soba dumplings before going into deep meditation or long fasts.

Ariko Inaoka, the 16th-generation (and first female) owner of her family restaurant, Honke Owariya, which was founded in 1465, says: 'Soba is a very spiritual food. Monks would eat the noodles as their last meal before going on a ten-day fast. It doesn't make your body feel heavy or tired – it's a very special kind of food.'

By the beginning of the Edo period in the 17th century, every neighbourhood of Edo (Tokyo) had at least one soba restaurant, the kind of place offering a casual meal with sake. Initially, soba was not considered to be as special as udon, which attracted a more wealthy clientele, probably because of the relatively cheap cost of buckwheat, but it gained popularity as a favourite quick and economical meal among the Edoites in the 1700s, helped on by the spread of mobile soba vendors, which operated at all hours of the night when other restaurants had closed.

There is a story that this love of soba even helped save the people of Edo from beri beri, a deficiency in Vitamin B1, which had been plaguing the poor people in rural communities who ate only white rice. Because buckwheat is so rich in Vitamin B, the soba-loving city folk were spared.

By the next century, the cost of buckwheat had gone up and, as Naomichi Ishige puts it in *History of Japanese Food*: 'Splendidly equipped soba shops emerged where persons of rank would eat.' Today, you could still say that soba is the preferred noodle of the Tokyoites, the noodle chosen for everyday meals, as it is so quick, light and refreshing. ●

'Soba is a very spiritual food. Monks would eat the noodles as their last meal before going on a ten-day fast. It doesn't make your body feel heavy or tired – it's a very special kind of food.'

–

ARIKO INAOKA
OF HONKE OWARIYA

粉

ON RAMEN

ラーメンについて

You may notice there is one thing missing in this book that has become incredibly popular outside of Japan: ramen. Ramen noodles in a big bowl of hearty broth is still not something my Japanese family are particularly into, at least not as much as soba, and since it isn't considered home cooking, it's not something I ate at home much either. When we did buy ramen noodles, it was to make yakisoba – which is misleading, as you would think it is meant to be made with soba noodles.

Ramen is a relatively new arrival on Japan's culinary scene. Thought to have been brought over by Chinese immigrants after the Meiji restoration in 1868, by 1910 Tokyo's first ramen shop had opened. Ramen, for most Japanese, is a very quick, cheap, practically 'fast food' lunch option when you're not at home. In fact, ramen shops have their beginnings in yatai, wooden carts on the street that offered ready-made meals of noodles, mochi and grilled eel, for example, day and night to busy workers, in particular to single men who comprised one and a half times the population of females in 19th-century Tokyo, or Edo, as it was known then.

I can remember during my student days appreciating the little standing-only ramen joints where you punch what you want into a machine beforehand, pay with coins, then it spits out a ticket that you take up to the counter – a very spartan, no-nonsense, tiny eatery that fits a handful of people. The size is not really a problem since you are in and out so quickly. The noodles come out in a flash, they are warm and filling and everything you need in a quick meal. I stand there attempting to slurp the way the others are, in their booths, facing the wall, but I'm just not as well-practised. ●

149

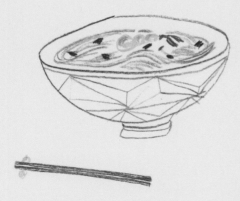

物

粉

New Year's Soba

年
越
し
そ
ば

Despite my long introduction to this beloved dish, this is a relatively quick meal to put together. I wanted to include this recipe because this is a dish I like to make every New Year's Eve (and not only then).

The New Year celebration is so important in Japanese culture and so – of course – the food is too, much like Christmas is in Western cultures. Colourful and symbolic dishes are made to celebrate health and good fortune in a meal called Osechi Ryori. These special foods can take days to prepare in advance. They get packed into lacquered boxes called jubako, that are stacked on top of each other in a few layers, to share with the whole family on New Year's Day.

Living so far away from my family in Australia and Japan, I don't get to have Osechi Ryori often, but I started making it myself to feel closer to my mother as she was preparing hers. We would swap messages about what we were making, what she is putting in her jubako this year, how she makes Namasu (page 118) and reminiscing about Obaachan's kuromame (sweet black beans – still one of my favourite things ever). But I soon realised it was like preparing a whole Christmas meal for myself (my sommelier husband is always working on New Year's Eve and unfortunately some of these very special dishes aren't favourites of my children – yet) and eventually I scaled things down to just toshikoshi soba, and it is a tradition that has stuck. It is so easy to prepare and even easier to eat.

The tradition of eating this dish for New Year's Eve dates back to old Edo, when it was said that eating soba noodles, which cut very easily with the teeth, represents letting go of the past, and because buckwheat can survive under harsh conditions, it also represents resilience for the coming year – all things that I can get behind as we go into a new year.

151

Cont. >

物

METHOD

Carefully remove the heads and shells of the prawns, but leave the tails on. Remove the dark digestive tract with a skewer or a toothpick, pulling it out rather than cutting down the spine. You can help them keep their shape by making some small incisions along the belly side so they won't curl up when cooking. Coat in a sprinkling of the flour (the rest you will use for the batter) and set aside.

Make a batter by mixing the rest of the flour with the measured cold water (my mother likes to use sparkling water). Don't over-mix and don't worry if there are lumps. Let the mixture chill in the fridge until needed.

Prepare the spinach by blanching in boiling salted water for no more than 1 minute, or until wilted. Drain and plunge into ice-cold water to stop the cooking. Squeeze out any excess water very well, then chop into 4 equal portions and set aside.

To make the broth, bring the ingredients to a simmer in a pan, then keep warm.

Prepare a small-medium pan that can hold the prawns in their entire length with enough vegetable oil so that the prawns can float (a depth of about 5 cm/2 in). Heat over a medium–high heat until the temperature comes to about 170°C (338°F). It should be ready when a drop of the batter is immediately surrounded by many tiny, vigorous little bubbles.

Make the tempura prawns by dipping the prawns, from the tail end, into the cold batter, then into the hot oil. Fry for about 1 minute or until the batter is crisp and puffed. You could do two at a time. They shouldn't brown, but stay pale in colour. Transfer with a slotted spoon to drain on a wire rack while you fry the others. While you are doing this, catch any little drips and blobs of batter that land in the oil before they turn brown – scooping them out with a slotted spoon or a spider and transferring them to drain on kitchen paper – these are called tenkasu and should never go to waste, they add fluffiness to okonomiyaki and takoyaki and make a favourite topping for noodles, too. In fact, you could sprinkle them into this soba as well.

Put a pan of water (no need to salt) on to boil for the noodles. Cook the noodles according to the packet instructions (it's usually less than 5 minutes). When ready, drain the noodles (in soba restaurants, the cooking water is precious, it is called sobayu and makes a delicious warm drink that is served at the end of the meal). Rinse them briefly in a bowl of cool water (or plunge in a bowl of ice-cold water if preparing cold noodles) to stop the cooking and tighten the noodle.

Immediately divide the soba among four deep soup bowls. Pour over the hot broth, top with a portion of blanched spinach and a fried prawn, then sprinkle over the spring onions. Serve right away. If you like heat, add some shichimi togarashi.

INGREDIENTS

4 extra-large raw prawns
   (jumbo shrimp)
50 g (⅓ cup) plain (all-purpose) flour
80 ml (⅓ cup) chilled water
160 g (5½ oz) spinach
salt
vegetable oil, for frying
200 g (7 oz) soba noodles
2 spring onions (scallions),
   finely chopped
shichimi togarashi (optional)

BROTH

1.125 litres (4½ cups) Dashi
   (page 30)
375 ml (1½ cups) Mentsuyu sauce
   (page 32)

粉

VARIATIONS

Soba is such a versatile dish – you can serve it hot or cold, you can keep this as simple as you like as a light meal or add some heartier elements (marinated duck breast is a classic) or seasonal vegetables. I particularly love sansai soba, which is similarly served in a broth but with seasonal wild mountain vegetables, like ferns and bamboo shoots; and, in hot weather, zaru soba, which is cold soba topped with some shredded nori with the cold dipping sauce on the side (don't forget a bit of wasabi and grated ginger or daikon). Vegetarians can use a kombu dashi and leave out the prawns or replace them with Kakiage, tempura vegetable fritters on page 154). Whichever way you go, don't forget to practise your slurping as you bring the noodles and their sauce to your mouth – it is truly the most practical way to eat them without getting sauce all over the place and more enjoyable, too.

NOTE

The most traditional Tokyo-style soba is made with 2 parts wheat flour to 8 parts buckwheat flour, known as 2:8 in Japanese, or ni-hachi. You should look for soba that is made with a majority of buckwheat flour – you can even find soba made with 100 per cent buckwheat, which is a gluten-free noodle. For more about the traditional Japanese New Year meal, Namiko Chen has an incredible resource for making a full Osechi Ryori on her blog, *Just One Cookbook*, and in a dedicated ebook.

物

Tempura Vegetable Fritters

MAKES 8 PIECES

かき揚げ

These are small tempura fritters made with mixed vegetables that are delicious on their own or in a bowl of soba or udon noodles, where they soak up the sauce. You can use any vegetables you like really, just cut them into small pieces so they cook quickly. Corn, green beans, edamame, shishito peppers or bell peppers, for example, all go well here. You can eat these alone with some grated daikon and soy sauce sweetened with a splash of mirin, or try them dipped in matcha salt: mix 1 teaspoon of salt with 1 teaspoon of powdered matcha.

154

METHOD

Mix the flour with the measured chilled water (my mother likes to use sparkling water). Don't over-mix and don't worry if there are lumps. Let the mixture chill in the fridge until needed.

Add the vegetables to the batter. You can drop in a couple of ice cubes if it hasn't had much time to chill.

Prepare a small-medium pan with enough vegetable oil so the kakiage can float (a depth of about 5 cm/2 in). Heat over a medium–high heat until the temperature comes to about 170°C (338°F). It should be ready when a drop of the batter is immediately surrounded by many tiny, vigorous little bubbles.

Make the kakiage by dropping tablespoons (or use chopsticks) of the vegetables in batter into the hot oil. Fry for about 1½–2 minutes, or until the batter is crisp and puffed. You can do several at a time, but don't crowd the pan. They shouldn't brown, but stay pale in colour. Transfer with a slotted spoon to drain on a wire rack while you fry the others.

If not using right away for noodles, keep these in an airtight container in the fridge until needed. You can re-fry them to crisp them up again if you want to, but I find that if you are using them for soup just nestle them into the hot broth as they are and they will warm through in the soup.

INGREDIENTS

75 g (½ cup) plain (all-purpose) flour
125 ml (½ cup) chilled water
½ small onion, thinly sliced
1 carrot, peeled and sliced into matchsticks
4 shishito peppers (or ¼ green bell pepper/capsicum), seeds removed, thinly sliced
vegetable oil, for frying

粉

物

Udon Noodles in Broth

SERVES 4

月
見
う
ど
ん

156

INGREDIENTS

2 teaspoons salt
200 ml (7 fl oz) water
400 g (2⅔ cups) plain (all-purpose)
  flour, plus extra for dusting

TO SERVE

1.125 litres (4½ cups) Dashi (page 30)
375 ml (1½ cups) Mentsuyu sauce
  (page 32)
1–2 spring onions (scallions),
  finely chopped
4 egg yolks
sprinkle of shichimi togarashi
  or sesame seeds (optional)

Tsukimi means 'moon viewing' and refers to the addition of a raw egg yolk, that looks like a shining full moon. It is named for the mid-autumn (fall) harvest moon when it was traditional to prepare this, but I crave it all year round. You can make it with store-bought fresh, frozen or dried udon, but with this simple preparation I want to share how to make fresh udon at home. If you've made fresh pasta at home before, then this is even easier, and there really is nothing like freshly made noodles.

METHOD

Dissolve the salt in the water in a large bowl. Add the flour and combine until you have a shaggy dough – you should be able to pick up any traces of flour with the dough. Transfer to a clean, dry surface and knead for 10–15 minutes. This involves quite a bit of elbow grease, but you don't have to move fast, just keep kneading. If your wrists get tired, it's common to put the dough in a ziplock bag, put on a pair of clean socks and knead the dough through the bag with the heel and balls of your feet. Otherwise, knead by hand until the surface of the dough is smooth and soft. Cover or place in an airtight container and leave to rest for at least 1–2 hours, the longer the better (even overnight).

With a rolling pin on a lightly dusted surface (wood is best), roll out the rested dough into a rectangle about 2 mm (⅛ in) thick. If you find it is retracting as you are trying to roll it out, the dough needs a bit more time to rest. Cover with a damp clean dish towel so it doesn't dry out and try again in 10 minutes. Lightly dust the top of the dough, then roll it or fold it over itself, lengthways, dusting well with flour between folds. Use a very sharp, large knife to cut the dough into 2 mm (⅛ in) thick slices. Do several at a time, then unroll carefully, and dust the freshly cut noodles in more flour. Set aside in a single layer on a tray lined with baking paper while you cut the rest.

Warm the dashi and mentsuyu sauce together in a small pan and keep warm.

Bring a pan of water to the boil (no need to salt it) and cook the noodles for 7–8 minutes, or until they no longer taste of flour but aren't mushy – they should have a good chew to them. Drain and rinse them in a bowl of cool water to give them a bit more bounce and bite, then drain again.

Distribute the noodles among four bowls, top with the hot broth and scatter over the spring onions. Nestle an egg yolk in the top of each bowl. Add some shichimi togarashi or sesame seeds, if you like.

VARIATIONS

If you don't like raw egg, try poached or fried instead, or leave out. Like soba, udon can be enjoyed in so many ways: I love kitsune or 'fox' udon, which is served with fried tofu (the name comes from its golden brown colour) or tempura prawn and prepared like the Toshikoshi soba (page 151), or using vegetable Kakiage (page 154) instead of the egg yolk. You can even put udon in a curry sauce (see page 216) – just make the sauce a little brothier by adding extra dashi or water. Or, when it's too hot to eat warm noodles, enjoy chilled.

粉

物

Cold Somen Noodles with Cucumber and Ginger

SERVES 4

そうめん

I crave this refreshing, light, but incredibly satisfying, cold dish in the hot, humid days of summer. It is the perfect thing when it's too hot to cook or too hot to eat. The slippery, silky, impossibly thin noodles coated with that delicious, sweet mentsuyu sauce just slide down your throat with no effort. I adore it. My mother puts ice cubes in the dish, too, which I think is the best touch.

158

METHOD

Prepare a bowl of ice-cold water while bringing a pan of unsalted water to the boil. Cook the somen noodles according to the packet instructions, then drain and plunge into the ice-cold water. Drain again and distribute among four shallow bowls.

Pour over the mentsuyu with the ginger stirred into it. Scatter over the cucumber strips, sesame seeds and spring onions, along with any of the other suggestions listed below. Add some ice cubes right before serving.

MORE ADDITIONS

This is really a blank canvas for you to paint with whatever you have on hand. Here are some of my other favourite additions to build on this: soft-boiled eggs, strips of ham, prawns (shrimp) or poached chicken to make it a bit more substantial, wasabi or shichimi togarashi for heat, halved cherry tomatoes for some extra umami, grated daikon, poached bok choy (pak choy) or spinach, watercress, or some more aromatics, such as finely chopped shiso leaf or a good drizzle of sesame oil.

INGREDIENTS

400 g (14 oz) dried somen noodles
375 ml (1½ cups) Mentsuyu sauce
  (page 32)
4 cm (1½ in) piece of fresh root ginger,
  finely grated
1 long Japanese cucumber, cut into
  thin, matchstick-length strips
1 teaspoon toasted sesame seeds
2 spring onions (scallions), thinly sliced
ice cubes, to serve

粉

物

粉

This is one of my very favourite dishes to make at home and because I don't always have calamari or the other seafood lying around that you normally see in this dish, I often make it with just cabbage (the one ingredient that is non-negotiable), like my mother does. One day, I added some cheese to it, and the stringy, cheesy interior was so good, it has now become my go-to.

Because it's hard to make okonomiyaki for more than one person, unless you have multiple pans going at once, I like making just one quite large one and then cutting it into wedges to share at the table – two hungry people would be very happy with this portion alone or you can easily stretch it out to share among more with some other little dishes. Otherwise, this is my favourite meal to make myself when I have a rare moment alone. Just halve it and it's the perfect meal for one.

It makes a great pantry dish and if you are wondering what else you can add to this, prawns (shrimp) and calamari or pork belly are popular proteins, but you can try other vegetables like mushrooms, beansprouts, even corn or kimchi. If you happen to have some tempura crumbs (see tenkasu, page 154), add a handful of these in here, too – it's not only traditional, but they help make it fluffier.

Cheese and Cabbage Okonomiyaki

SERVES 2 GENEROUSLY

お
好
み
焼
き

161

METHOD

Make a batter by mixing the flour, baking powder, egg yolks and dashi. Rest the batter for about 30 minutes.

Meanwhile, beat the egg whites until you have firm peaks.

After the resting time, fold the egg whites into the batter along with the pickled ginger.

Grease a large, heavy-based frying pan (skillet) (cast-iron is great as it holds the heat well and cooks evenly) and heat over a low–medium heat. Spread half of the batter mixture out in the pan, sprinkle over half of the cheese, then layer over the cabbage, top with the rest of the cheese, then pour over the remaining batter. Cover and cook for 5 minutes.

Remove the lid and carefully flip the okonomiyaki over. I find what works best is either 2 spatulas and some good manoeuvring, or do it like an Italian frittata: use an inverted plate, clamp that down over the okonomiyaki, then flip the whole pan over onto the plate. Finally, slide the okonomiyaki, now flipped, back into the pan on the raw side. Cover and cook for a final 5 minutes.

Place on a plate and garnish with some drizzles of tonkatsu sauce and Japanese mayonnaise, then sprinkle over aonori and katsuobushi. Place the beni shoga in the centre. Serve cut into wedges if you like, or just dig in with chopsticks.

INGREDIENTS

60 g (2 oz) plain (all-purpose) flour
1 teaspoon baking powder
2 eggs, separated
80 ml (⅓ cup) Kombu dashi (page 30) or water
2 tablespoons Beni shoga (red pickled ginger, page 36)
vegetable oil, for greasing
70 g (2½ oz) good melting cheese, shredded or in thin slices
350 g (12½ oz) cabbage (about ⅓ head of cabbage), finely sliced

GARNISHES

Tonkatsu sauce (page 34)
Japanese mayonnaise
aonori (green seaweed flakes)
katsuobushi (dried bonito flakes)
Beni shoga (red pickled ginger, page 36)

物

Fried Noodles

SERVES 4

焼
き
そ
ば

Yakisoba (which, despite its name, is made with ramen noodles not soba noodles) is a dish I grew up on and it makes an excellent weeknight meal – quick, satisfying, and something you can make without too many special requirements or with whatever you have in the fridge. Saying that, there are certain vegetables that belong here and give the dish its unique flavour. For me, cabbage is an absolute must, along with the sweetness of carrot. Some type of mushroom, such as shiitake, dried or fresh, or any other Asian mushrooms, such as king brown or oyster, lend deep flavour. Other seasonal green vegetables, such as peas, green beans or broccoli, are great in here, too. You can even add a small amount of thinly sliced beef, pork belly or even bacon or ham, if you wish. The egg is my favourite part, so I personally never leave it out – sometimes I just scramble it, but a whole fried one is quite irresistible. You can also use udon noodles instead of ramen noodles.

I've listed some optional garnishes below, but in reality one of them is not an option, it is a *must* – beni shoga, these punchy pink ginger pickles are the ultimate foil to the sweet yakisoba sauce!

If you cannot find tonkatsu sauce, then try the quick or longer solutions on page 34, but – in a pinch – you can use some Worcestershire sauce in its place (you may need a dash more sugar to balance out its sharpness, as tonkatsu sauce is on the sweet side). Vegetarians only need to leave out the oyster sauce and perhaps balance out with the sugar (I quite like brown sugar in this case).

INGREDIENTS

SAUCE
2 tablespoons oyster sauce
2 tablespoons Tonkatsu sauce (page 34)
2 tablespoons tomato ketchup
1 tablespoon soy sauce
1 teaspoon sugar

NOODLES
200 g (7 oz) dried ramen noodles (500 g/1 lb 2 oz fresh)
2–3 mushrooms (shiitake, for example)
1 tablespoon sesame oil
¼ head of cabbage, finely sliced
½ small onion, thinly sliced
¼ green bell pepper (capsicum), thinly sliced
1 carrot, peeled and cut into matchsticks
50 g (1¾ oz/a handful) mung bean sprouts
4 eggs
1 spring onion (scallion), finely chopped

OPTIONAL GARNISHES
Beni shoga (red pickled ginger, page 36), toasted sesame seeds, aonori (green seaweed flakes) or dried nori seaweed cut into strips, katsuobushi (dried bonito flakes)

METHOD

Combine the sauce ingredients and set aside.

If using dried noodles, boil as instructed on the packet and drain. Blanch fresh noodles in boiling water for 30 seconds, then drain. For both, shock the drained noodles in a bowl of cool water, then drain again. Set aside.

If using dried mushrooms, leave them to soak in hot water until they are 'revived' and soft, about 20 minutes. Slice thinly.

Heat a wide pan or wok over a medium–high heat with half of the sesame oil. Add the cabbage, onion, green pepper, carrot and mushrooms, and toss, cooking until the cabbage is wilted and the carrot cooked but still with a bit of bite, about 7 minutes. Tip in the noodles and mung bean sprouts, followed by the sauce. Toss everything together for a moment, until the sauce coats the noodles. You may need to add a splash of water to keep it shiny.

Remove from the heat but keep warm while you fry the eggs in the rest of the sesame oil for 1–2 minutes, or until the edges are frilly and the whites are set but the yolk is still runny.

Serve immediately with the chopped spring onion, garnishes of choice and the fried egg on top.

162

粉

物

粉

Prawn Balls

MAKES 28

海
老
焼
き

Originating in 1930s Osaka, this beloved street-food dish is better known as takoyaki (たこ焼き) – *tako* meaning 'octopus' and *yaki* being the general word for grilling. *Ebi* is 'prawn' (shrimp) and I prefer this version for a couple of reasons: mainly, it's easier to use prawns at home, you don't have to cook them first and they are relatively easy to prepare and buy – a bit less daunting than a large octopus. Not to mention they are absolutely delicious.

The key to the characteristic crisp-on-the-outside, creamy-on-the-inside texture (sotokari nakatoro is how it is described in Japanese) is the batter, which is almost like a savoury crêpe batter, made simply with flour, eggs and dashi. My friend and fellow Australian cookbook author Adam Liaw uses a very liquid batter with about 1 litre (4 cups) of dashi, while Japanese-American chef Niki Nakayama uses a thicker batter with less than a cup of dashi. I like to go somewhere in between, but the more fluid batter makes it easier to shape these little balls.

You'll notice the garnishes are the same as for okonomiyaki and, similarly, if you happen to have some tempura crumbs (see tenkasu, page 154), it is traditional to add a handful of these in here, too, as they help make them fluffier.

Cont. >

物

INGREDIENTS

150 g (1 cup) plain (all-purpose) flour
2 eggs
500 ml (2 cups) Dashi (page 30)
500 g (1 lb 2 oz) raw prawns (shrimp)
     (about 150 g/5 oz,
     if already peeled)
3 spring onions (scallions),
     finely chopped
1–2 tablespoons Beni shoga (red
     pickled ginger, page 36)
1 tablespoon vegetable oil

GARNISHES

Tonkatsu sauce (page 34)
Japanese mayonnaise
aonori (green seaweed flakes)
katsuobushi (dried bonito flakes)

NOTE

You do need special equipment for
making these, namely a pan with little
hemispheres hollowed into it. There are
actually a number of things on the
market that are for completely different
preparations but that are essentially the
exact contraption you need: try a Dutch
or Danish pancake pan (poffertjes or
aebleskiver, respectively), or even a cake
pop–maker. These are simply pans (often
cast-iron) that you place over your regular
stove-top heat source, but the cake pop–
maker tends to be electric. Personally,
I think you could get creative with a waffle
maker too – they won't be ball-shaped
but they would be very fun.

METHOD

Make the batter by mixing the flour and eggs, then stir in the dashi.
You should have a very fluid, smooth batter.

Remove the heads and shells of the prawns if they are whole and slice
down the back with a sharp knife to remove the digestive tract. Chop into
1–2 cm (½–¾ in) pieces and set aside, along with the spring onions and
the beni shoga.

Heat a takoyaki pan (or similar) over a medium heat. With a pastry brush
or with the help of some absorbent kitchen paper, grease the holes of the
pan. Ladle or pour over some of the batter to fill each hole almost to the top,
immediately followed by a scattering of prawns (a couple of pieces in each
hole), spring onion and beni shoga. Top up with some more of the batter –
this should overflow and cover the pan completely (you will see there is a lip
on the edge to catch it all). Cook for 1–2 minutes.

Next, with the help of two skewers or pointed Japanese chopsticks, you are
going to shape the batter into balls. The easiest way to do this is to first cut
a 'grid' in the overflowed batter around each of the holes, then roll the balls
with a quarter turn, poking in the excess batter that had overflowed to fill
the space left inside the hole. Wait a minute, then use the skewers to do
another quarter turn – the pan should now be filled with nicely browned
little spheres. Keep turning in quarters, giving them another minute or two
until they are evenly browned. In total, this can take about 5–6 minutes.
If you notice the holes in the middle are cooking faster than the ones on the
edge, for example, remove the cooked balls from the pan and transfer to
a plate, then shift the outer balls into the centre so they are evenly browned.

Decorate the plate of ebiyaki with drizzles of tonkatsu sauce and
Japanese mayonnaise and a sprinkling of aonori and katsuobushi flakes
(or any combination of those that you like).

VARIATIONS

You could try other fillings too, such as bacon or ham, even cheese.
Vegetarians can use kombu dashi for these and replace the prawns with
some vegetables – my picks would be chopped cabbage (these taste like
mini okonomiyaki and are a common addition to Tokyo-style takoyaki),
peas, edamame or even corn kernels.

粉

物

Salted Grilled Chicken Skewers

MAKES 16

塩
焼
き
鳥

168

A classic street food and one found also in yakitori-ya (special yakitori shops) or in izakaya (Japanese bars serving food), yakitori can be made with all parts of the chicken – heart, gizzards, the 'parson's nose' (the tail) – you name it, there is a skewer for it. You can also do this with chicken breast, but my preference is the thigh – it is juicier and more flavourful. It's also very good with the skin left on, which can get delicious and crisp here. Yakitori is usually either just salted (shio) or enhanced after cooking with a lick of tare (sauce), such as teriyaki, but my mother always made them with just salt. It's incredible how delicious only a few ingredients can be together.

For the spring onions (scallions), traditionally negi are used, which are thicker than regular spring onions with a longer white section, which is the part I love best – it can withstand longer cooking than the green part and turns deliciously sweet when cooked this way. Save the green tops for when you need some garnish for another dish.

INGREDIENTS

¼–½ teaspoon salt
700 g (1 lb 9 oz) skin-on chicken thighs, cut into thin strips
1–2 tablespoons sake, if you have it
6–8 spring onions (scallions), cut into 2.5 cm (1 in) sections, use mainly the white parts

NOTE

If cooking over a barbecue and using wooden skewers rather than metal, it is a good idea to soak the skewers in water for about 10 minutes before using, to prevent burning.

METHOD

Salt the chicken thighs and rub it all over to distribute well. If you have sake, adding a splash here will help add umami and keep the chicken tender. Thread the chicken, alternating with the spring onions, onto 16 skewers.

Heat a cast-iron grill pan or, even better, directly over a charcoal barbecue on high heat. Cook the skewers, turning regularly so that all sides cook evenly, about 10 minutes in total.

粉

物

FAMILY FAVOURITES

お気に入

This is the chapter that makes me think of family eating, gathering around a hotpot or getting fingers sticky eating chicken wings as children – many of the recipes here are dishes that I've loved since childhood that I have now passed on to my own family. These are the kind of dishes you may not necessarily find in a restaurant (although some appear in specialty restaurants and even in konbini, convenience stores) but you certainly would at home. Many of these also happen to make great components of a bento box, even cold the next day.

Nabemono, or nabe for short, are generally wintery dishes of meat, tofu and vegetables, sometimes even noodles, cooked hotpot-style in a bubbling sauce or broth (*nabe*, in fact, is the name of the cooking pot, and *mono* simply means 'thing'). These are usually cooked directly at the table with a portable gas or induction burner. It may seem like a big, clunky, unnecessary thing to have in addition to your regular stove, but there is nothing quite like having the pot in the middle of the table, bubbling away, with everyone gathered around it and many Japanese households have one. We always grew up with one, but they are getting even sleeker and slimmer now to fit into the tiniest of kitchens to have the option of making dishes like Sukiyaki (page 177), shabu shabu (a similar dish, but cooked in a simpler dashi broth and served with dipping sauces) and Oden (page 183) on the table, but even takoyaki or Ebiyaki (page 165) – and why not, anything else you might want to grill or cook right in the middle of the table?

It's a very social, interactive way of cooking and eating and probably my favourite welcome home meal for this reason. The ultimate of these kind of dishes for me is Sukiyaki – one of my favourites when we are at my mother's, it was also a signature dish of Obaachan – a delicious dashi- and soy-based sauce, and a huge platter of vegetables, shirataki noodles, tofu and paper-thin slices of raw beef are at the ready for cooking – and eating – together around the pot with individual bowls of rice. ●

Eating snacks with my grandfather.

メニュー

JAPANESE
COOKING TECHNIQUES

和
食
作
り
の
テ
ク
ニ
ッ
ク

SIMMERING

The technique of simmering (known as ni) in Japanese home cooking is one of the two most important techniques, along with grilling (or broiling, known as yaki). Nimono literally means 'simmered things' and usually refers to vegetables, meat, fish or tofu simmered in a shiru, or a lightly flavoured dashi-based stock. Unlike in Western cuisines, most Japanese stews and simmered dishes are not intended for long, slow cooking – aroma, flavour and texture are preserved through shorter cooking times. Similarly, soups, such as miso soup and clear soups and broth for noodles, also don't take long to prepare, because too much cooking can ruin the flavour of kombu or miso and even vegetables are usually cut into thin matchsticks or thin slices for quick cooking.

GRILLING AND FRYING

The word for 'grilled' in Japanese, *yaki*, literally means 'cooking over direct heat' and can also be roughly translated as 'pan-fried' (or perhaps some might call it 'stir-fried', even though this isn't strictly a Japanese cooking technique), but it also encompasses the equivalent of baking, roasting, broiling (such as under the top part of an electric oven) or grilling/barbecuing over gas or coals.

In fact, you'll see it in the names of some of the cuisine's most well-known dishes and sauces, from teppanyaki to yakitori to okonomiyaki. Next to simmering, yaki is one of the main techniques used for cooking in a Japanese home. Growing up, many of my very favourite childhood dishes were cooked this way: sweet soy chicken wings (which we actually bake rather than cook on a stove top – oven baking isn't traditional in Japan as you can read more about on page 23), big 'pancakes' of okonomiyaki filled with shredded cabbage, and yakisoba, noodles tossed in a pan with quickly cooked vegetables and egg (or whatever was on hand) in a sweet and vinegary soy sauce; also – a must for my ideal Japanese breakfast – grilled fish.

Deep-frying, known as *age* (pronounced 'ah-ghe'), is a different term and technique from yaki – and also not traditionally Japanese. Battering and deep-frying is a technique that was introduced to Japan by the Portuguese in the 16th century and adopted and adapted to suit local tastes. The Japanese are quite sensitive about food being greasy, so deep-frying at the right temperature is important for sealing the food from the outside so that essentially it is steam that is doing the cooking and the resulting food doesn't feel heavy. Satsumaage (fried fish cakes, page 186), Kakiage (tempura vegetable fritters, page 154) and Karaage (fried chicken, page 196) are some of my favourite Japanese fried foods that I love making at home. These foods are often served with grated daikon radish or raw cabbage to aid digestion. ●

お気に入

メニュー

お気に入

This dish has a special place in my heart. It was everyone's favourite signature dish of my obaachan, and one of the rare occasions she would cook meat. It felt like such a special treat and still is for me when my mother makes it. I've lived continents away from home since going to university; after being away for a year, sukiyaki was the dish (along with Temaki – page 97 – if it was summertime) that my mother would make to welcome me home.

Invented in the Meiji era, after the Emperor dropped the 1,200-year-old ban on meat, sukiyaki was a dish that encouraged the Japanese to embrace eating beef. We make sukiyaki in the Kanto (Tokyo) style, where the sauce goes in first and everything is simmered in it, then taken out as each ingredient is cooked. In Kansai style (around Osaka), the meat is grilled first in the pot, usually with some beef tallow to grease it, and can be savoured as is, followed by the sauce and vegetables.

Starting with a sweet sauce of mirin, sake and soy sauce, simmering right at the table, you place the well-marbled, paper-thin slices of beef into the sauce, along with vegetables, tofu and shirataki noodles. Every ingredient takes on the most wonderful flavours and everyone has their favourites. (Mine?... The tofu, which is like a sponge that soaks up that sauce, and the spring onion, which becomes impossibly sweet – I love it so much I make an easy version of it to eat anytime, see page 138.)

Guests are served bowls of rice and bowls with a single raw egg cracked into them. You beat the egg with your chopsticks and it serves as a dipping sauce for the boiling-hot foods coming straight out of the pot. As the hot, saucy meat or vegetables hits the raw egg, it becomes a deliciously, creamy sauce – think carbonara – and it is one of my favourite parts of this dish.

Cont. >

Welcome Home Sukiyaki

SERVES 4

すき焼き

177

This dish has a special place in my heart. I've lived continents away from home since going to university; after being away for a year, sukiyaki was the dish that my mother would make to welcome me home.

INGREDIENTS

300 g (10½ oz) marbled beef
   (such as sirloin), very thinly sliced
1 block of medium-firm tofu, cut into
   1.5 cm (½ in) slices
2–4 spring onions (scallions) or
   1 leek, cut on the diagonal into
   5 cm (2 in) pieces
1 pack of enoki mushrooms
4 king oyster mushrooms,
   sliced lengthways
1 small head of napa cabbage,
   chopped into 2.5 cm (1 in) segments
1 large bunch of shungiku
   chrysanthemum greens, or similar,
   cut into 5 cm (2 in) sections
200 g (7 oz) shirataki noodles
4 bowls of freshly cooked Japanese
   short-grain rice (page 80)
4 very fresh eggs, for dipping (optional)

SUKIYAKI SAUCE
125 ml (½ cup) mirin
125 ml (½ cup) sake
125 ml (½ cup) soy sauce
2 tablespoons sugar, or to taste
125 ml (½ cup) water

METHOD

To make the sukiyaki sauce, place the mirin and sake in a saucepan and bring to the boil, which will evaporate the alcohol. After 2 minutes, turn down to a gentle simmer and add the soy sauce, sugar and water and continue simmering, stirring occasionally, until the sugar is dissolved. Set aside. (You can make this in advance and keep in a jar in the fridge for up to a week.)

To prepare the table for sukiyaki, set up the burner in the centre of the table with the pot of sauce on top (sukiyaki is normally cooked in a cast-iron pot). Arrange the beef on a platter and arrange the tofu, vegetables and shirataki noodles attractively on a separate platter. Serve each guest a bowl of rice, a bowl with a freshly cracked egg, if using, and some chopsticks.

Turn on the burner and bring the sauce to a simmer over a low–medium heat. Add the meat and some of the vegetables (enough to fit – you'll do a few rounds). Pick out the ingredients as they are ready – most things take mere minutes to cook: the tofu and greens are very quick; the cabbage, leek or spring onions can go longer, for example.

To avoid contamination of chopsticks in the sukiyaki, rather than allow every guest to use their own chopsticks, use a pair of saibashi, cooking chopsticks, which are longer than regular chopsticks, that stays by the pot and anyone who wants to take something out can use those alone. Otherwise, appoint a 'cook' who is in charge of distributing the foods as they are ready to come out.

VARIATION

Simply leave out the beef and add a little extra of the other ingredients (my favourites are the tofu and the leek, but mushrooms are excellent in this dish, as they soak up the sauce so well); vegans only need to leave out the dipping egg, too.

お気に

ON THE INGREDIENTS

My mother eyeballs this recipe, so it is always a bit different each time, so when I asked her for her recipe she turned to one of her oldest and best friends, Chieko, who is also a brilliant cook, to share her recipe, which is just perfect. Sukiyaki sauce has a distinctly sweet flavour, and my mother likes to keep the sugar to a minimum – you could use a little less if you prefer, too.

Traditional ingredients in sukiyaki include shirataki noodles, which are gluten-free noodles made of yam starch; different types of Japanese mushrooms, such as enoki, fresh shiitake or oyster mushrooms; and chrysanthemum greens (shungiku, 春菊), which are confusingly not the leaves of chrysanthemum flowers but actually another plant that resembles them – they are deliciously bitter, and you could substitute another bitter green for them, or simply try spinach, bok choy (pak choy), broccoli rabe or even watercress. If you manage to find shungiku to include here, note that like spinach they cook very quickly and will only need about 30 seconds in the pot. The quality of the beef is important here and, for an occasion dish like this, it is worth splurging for – there isn't too much meat as it isn't the main star of the dish. Not only should it be good quality but it should also be well marbled so that it remains very tender. Recently, in Nagano, we enjoyed sukiyaki with a delicious wagyu particular to the region where the cows are fed only apples. My mother buys impossibly thin, pre-sliced frozen beef from her local Korean grocer and it is perfect for this, as the slices should be paper thin – about 2 mm or at most 3 mm (⅛ inch) thick. If you can't get the pre-sliced beef, choose a nice piece of marbled steak from your butcher, put it in the freezer to firm up for about 1–2 hours and then you should be able to slice it thinly.

179

メニュー

お気に入

メニュー

お気に入

Winter Hotpot

お
で
ん

This is the kind of dish that warms you from the inside on the coldest day of winter. It traditionally isn't considered a very refined dish – in fact, it used to be a dish you would find peddlers selling on the street and today you can even buy hot oden at konbini, convenience stores, hinting too at how affordable it is – but it is so comforting and pure soul food.

Its name means 'hodgepodge' and, in fact, each household will put a different combination of ingredients in their oden, but like sukiyaki and other soul-food dishes, there are certain ingredients that belong in this dish that give it is particular flavours and textures. Boiled eggs, konnyaku (a gelatinous yam cake appreciated for its chewy texture more than its flavour), daikon and a number of different shapes and types of fish cakes are what make this special. You might also find potatoes, carrots, satoimo (Japanese taro), miniature frankfurter sausages, or even pork ribs or chicken wings (although we never had meat in our oden growing up), which help make it filling and comforting. I also love the addition of mochi in here, sealed in a little fried aburaage tofu bag closed with a gourd drawstring (or toothpick) called mochi kinchaku – the chewiness of mochi in hot winter soups is something that sends me instantly into a haze of nostalgia.

See what you have and what you can get for your own oden. Although this is such a simple dish, it is probably one of the hardest for me to make outside of Japan, because the thing I love most about oden is also the thing I've never been able to find where I live: the nerimono, or fish cakes. They're often part of an 'oden kit' that you might be able to find in the freezer section of your local Asian grocer. Commonly, there would be things like chikuwa (a long, cigar-shaped fish cake with a hole through the middle like a straw), hanpen (a fluffy-textured nerimono made with yamato yam and fish) and satsumaage fish balls, which often have vegetables mixed through them, too. Feel free to include all of these, if you can get them. The more variety, the more flavour your oden will have.

Cont. >

183

メニュー

INGREDIENTS

BROTH

1 large piece of kombu,
 about 10 cm (4 in) square
1 litre (4 cups) water
1 teaspoon salt
80 ml (⅓ cup) soy sauce
2 tablespoons mirin

ODEN

250 g (9 oz) daikon
1 kirimochi (dried mochi),
 broken into 4 pieces
4 pieces of aburaage (fried tofu)
150 g (5½ oz) konnyaku (yam cake),
 scored and sliced into
 bite-sized triangles
8 Satsumaage (fried fish cakes,
 page 186)
2 small new potatoes,
 peeled and halved
1 carrot, peeled and chopped
 into thick slices
1 leek or 2–3 spring onions (scallions)
4 soft-boiled eggs, peeled (see note)
4 miniature frankfurter sausages
karashi mustard or shichimi togarashi,
 to serve (optional)

NOTE

To easily peel softly set boiled eggs
(I boil room-temperature eggs in
gently simmering water for 7 minutes),
it's helpful to start with older eggs – they
peel easier than fresher ones. Also, it's
easiest to peel them under water. Fill a
mixing bowl with some water, gently crack
the eggs all over on a hard surface, then
lower them into the water and try to peel
them while submerged.

METHOD

Make a kombu dashi by soaking the kombu in the measured water overnight
along with the salt. The next day, heat the dashi gently, but just before
it comes to the boil, turn off the heat. Remove the kombu and slice it into
2 cm (¾ in) strips. Tie each strip into a knot and set aside.

Because the daikon needs plenty of time to cook to be able to absorb
the flavours well, it's best to parboil it. Start by peeling and cutting it into
2 cm (¾ in) thick slices (and then into half moons, if very large). Score
an X in each piece on one side (this is called kakushi boucho or 'hidden cuts'
and helps the daikon cook more evenly). Parboil in a small pan of the
first washing of rice water if you have it, otherwise use plain water, for about
20 minutes. Drain and set aside.

Prepare the mochi kinchaku tofu pouches by placing a little piece of kirimochi
inside each aburaage 'pocket'. Seal the open side with a toothpick on each one.

Blanch the konnyaku in a small pan of boiling water to remove its odour.
As you are draining the water, pour it over the satsumaage to remove any
excess oil. Drain and set both foods aside.

Rinse the peeled potatoes to remove any excess starch.

Combine the kombu dashi with the soy sauce and mirin and bring to a simmer.
Lower in the vegetables and konnyaku first and cook for about 10–15 minutes,
covered. Add the mochi kinchaku, and the satsumaage, which shouldn't cook
for long or they will become too soft – 5 minutes, covered, should be enough.
If you like, you can place a skewer through the frankfurters for easy eating.
Add them, along with the boiled eggs, and simmer for 3 minutes.

Serve piping hot with karashi mustard or shichimi togarashi, if you like
a bit of heat.

Leftovers, gently reheated the next day, are arguably even tastier.

VARIATION

If you leave out the sausages and satsumaage, this is a delicious vegan hotpot
– you could use some tofu, shiitake or king oyster mushrooms in their place.

お気に入

メニュー

Fried Fish Cakes

MAKES 12 FISH CAKES

薩
摩
揚
げ

I adore all types of fish cakes, but especially satsumaage. I'm convinced it's in my DNA – my grandfather was originally from Kyushu, in southern Japan, where they are famous for these deep-fried fish cakes that he, too, loved. They got their name from this area, which today is known as Kagoshima, but was historically known as the Satsuma region. *Age* (pronounced 'ah-ghe') means 'fried thing'. I ended up making them myself for the first time many years ago when I was living in Florence, following Yumiko's recipe from the blog *RecipeTin Japan*, and found it was so easy to do and instantly satisfied my nostalgic cravings. They taste like home.

These are usually made with cod, but you can find many regional varieties with different fish, for example, yellowtail, mackerel, sardines, sea bass. Try combining two types of fish, if you can, for better flavour. Often, various vegetables are used in these, too: hijiki seaweed is popular to add a speckled appearance, shiitake, green beans, shiso for fresh fragrance, or lotus root for some crunch. You can even add cheese. They can be flat, oval, round like ping pong balls, cylinders and more. I shape them like the maruten that I remember my grandfather loved, which are round and flat like pancakes.

186

METHOD

Ensure there are no skin or bones on or in the fish. Place the fillets in a food processor with the salt, sake, egg white and just the juice of the grated ginger, not the fibrous part (I use a Japanese grating dish for this, then just squeeze the juice out with my fingers – you can also do this with a microplane and let the juice drip into the food processor). Blend to a paste. Add the carrot and onion and blend again until well combined, then stir through the potato starch.

Take 2 tablespoons of the mixture and, with wet or oiled hands, form into balls, then flatten slightly to patties about 1.5 cm (½ in) thick. Place them on a tray or a plate until all the mixture has been used up.

In a medium pan, heat enough vegetable oil for the fish cakes to float (a depth of about 5 cm/2 in). When it reaches about 170°C (338°F), fry the fish cakes in batches for about 3–4 minutes in total, until they are evenly golden brown on both sides. Drain on a wire rack lined with absorbent kitchen paper.

You can eat these just as they are, dipped in a little soy sauce, with grated daikon and lemon wedges, or use them in Oden (page 183).

INGREDIENTS

300 g (10½ oz) fish fillets,
   such as mackerel and sea bass
¼ teaspoon salt
1 teaspoon sake, if you have it
1 egg white
4 cm (1½ in) piece of fresh root ginger,
   peeled and grated
¼ carrot, peeled and finely chopped
½ onion, finely chopped
2 tablespoons potato starch
vegetable oil, for frying

お気に入

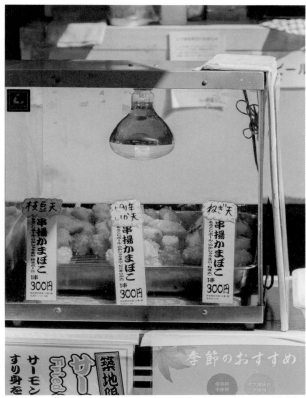

メニュー

Simmered Kingfish Stew

SERVES 4

ぶ
り
じ
や
が

For me, the flavour of daikon is the taste of Japanese home cooking. Bittersweet and earthy when cooked; an uplifting, bright digestif when raw, it is excellent in stews and soups as it draws in flavour like a sponge. It's no wonder it is the most-consumed vegetable in Japan. I love the combination of kingfish and daikon together, but you can also do this with beef or pork, too (if you do, slice the meat as thinly as you can, see the tips on the Sukiyaki recipe, page 179), and if you can't find daikon or it's not in season, simply leave it out.

In fact, this is the same braising sauce as for nikujaga, a delicious, homely Japanese beef and potato stew that every household will have their own recipe for. You may notice there is a relatively small amount of fish called for here, but in Japan the meat or fish in a stew is there to add flavour rather than be the star of the show and it is the root vegetables instead that soak up this flavour and become the best bits.

188

METHOD

Peel and cut the daikon into 2 cm (¾ in) thick slices and then into half moons (if it is a particularly large daikon, you may need to cut the slices into quarters). Score an X into one side of each slice and parboil for about 10 minutes while you prepare the rest of the dish. This removes any bitterness and gives it a headstart in the cooking process.

Cut the kingfish fillets into large chunks, about 5 cm (2 in) wide. Peel and cut the potatoes into similar-sized chunks as the daikon.

Place the daikon, potatoes and onion into a saucepan, pour over the dashi stock and bring to a gentle simmer, covered. After 15 minutes, immerse the pieces of kingfish in the stock and add the sake, mirin and soy sauce. Continue cooking gently for a further 10 minutes, uncovered, to allow the sauce to reduce a little, or until the vegetables are tender.

Serve with warm steamed rice and, if you like a bit of heat, sprinkle over some shichimi togarashi.

INGREDIENTS

1 piece of daikon
  (about 12 cm/4¾ in wide)
300 g (10½ oz) kingfish fillets,
  skin and bones removed
2–3 potatoes
1 small onion, sliced
250 ml (1 cup) Dashi (page 30)
2 tablespoons sake
2 tablespoons mirin
2 tablespoons soy sauce
Steamed rice (page 80), to serve
shichimi togarashi, to serve (optional)

お気に入

メニュー

お気に入

Marinated Fried Mackerel

SERVES 4

南
蛮
酢
け

191

This dish might even belong in the Yoshoku chapter, with the other Western–Japanese fusion dishes, but it is so old that, like tempura, it has been completely absorbed into the cuisine as a classic. The Portuguese explorers who arrived in Nagasaki in the 16th century introduced the preparation of marinating fried fish, escabeche, to the Japanese, who called it nanbanzuke (literally 'southern barbarian marinade'), and in fact nanbanzuke resembles any dish related to escabeche that you can still find today. The first time I had scaveccio, a local dish from the Tuscan lagoon town of Orbetello, I was shocked at the resemblance to nanbanzuke. Orbetello is famous for its eel, which is fished out of the lagoon, then cut into pieces that are floured, deep-fried and marinated in white wine vinegar, bay leaf, rosemary and chilli; it is still made this way at the local fishermen's cooperative. The dishes even date to a similar period, which is what connects them, along with an influence from the Spanish empire: 14 years after the Portuguese were the first Europeans to arrive in Japan, Orbetello came under Spanish rule.

My mother, Sumie, loves to make this in the summertime, as it is a dish that you can make in advance and keep in the fridge, pulling out for a chilled, uplifting meal when it is too hot to cook. I do, too. She likes to add plenty of lemon slices (like her pickled daikon, page 52) and use yellowtail for this, which is harder for me to find in Italy, but I love this with mackerel. You can also use sardines, salmon or chicken.

METHOD

Make sure there are no bones in the mackerel fillets – pull any small bones out with tweezers if there are any. Cut off any fins with scissors and dust the fillets completely in the potato starch.

Heat the olive oil in a medium frying pan (skillet) over a medium–high heat and shallow-fry the fish pieces for 1 minute on each side. Drain on a wire rack lined with kitchen paper, then sprinkle with salt and place in a deep ceramic or glass dish. Scatter over the carrot and onion.

Combine the marinade ingredients in a pan and simmer together for a few minutes to allow the alcohol to evaporate. Pour the hot marinade over the fish and vegetables. Add the lemon slices and chilli and leave to marinate for 30 minutes, or as long as you can wait to taste it – but it is even better the next day and lasts very well kept in the fridge for several days. For this reason, this is a generous serving, since it is a very good idea to have leftovers for the next day.

INGREDIENTS

300 g (10½ oz) mackerel fillets, cut into 4 cm (1½ in) pieces
2 tablespoons potato starch or plain (all-purpose) flour
2 tablespoons olive oil or other vegetable oil
salt
½ carrot, peeled and cut into matchsticks
½ onion, thinly sliced
1 lemon, thinly sliced
1 hot chilli, chopped

MARINADE
80 ml (⅓ cup) rice wine vinegar
3 tablespoons Dashi (page 30) or water
2 tablespoons soy sauce
2 tablespoons mirin
1 tablespoon sake

お気に入

HOW TO
PACK A BENTO BOX

お弁当箱の詰め方

Bento is a portable box of food for a meal on the run, whether it be for school, work or travel. Although bento may seem like a modern convenience, it actually dates back to the Edo period (1603–1868), when meals could be specially ordered for picnics and excursions.

There are several things that are important to packing a bento box, which haven't changed since that time and that also play a practical role:

RICE IS THE BASE

It is not only the staple for most meals, but it is also an excellent tool for soaking up any excess liquids and flavours from other elements in the bento.

ELEMENTS SHOULD BE TIGHTLY PACKED

This not only makes it look abundant, but filling the bento box to the top helps the ingredients stay in place during travel as they won't be able to jumble around.

ADD COLOUR

Not only should bento be attractive and fun (because we also eat with our eyes), but a range of colourful foods indicates variety, which means its nutritious too.

KEEPING FOOD SAFELY
WITHOUT REFRIGERATION IS IMPORTANT

Pack a fresh bento in the morning to be eaten at lunchtime and be aware of the food temperature (more on this below). Separating foods using leaves not only looks pretty, but can help to slow the spread of bacteria (when plants are cut or picked, they release antibacterial and antifungal substances known as phytoncides). Try bamboo or shiso leaves for example; persimmon and oak leaves, or anything in the allium family, have particularly high amounts of phytoncides.

Bento is usually eaten at room temperature, so a large part of enjoying bento is choosing foods that will still be delicious even if they're not piping hot or chilled. To ensure safety, it is best to pack the bento freshly in the morning – use freshly cooked rice as refrigerating rice ruins its texture (although you could reheat refrigerated rice by cooking it for fried rice like in the Chahan (page 102) or the Tamago no gohan (page 101) recipes – you could even prepare it as you would for omuraisu). Once you pack the hot rice in the bento, let it cool down to room temperature before packing the other fresh foods and closing the box.

Keep the box cool until you are ready to eat it. In warm weather, carry the bento in a refrigerator bag or keep an ice pack next to it – Japanese daiso (dollar stores/pound shops) are perfect for picking up these items.

Bento, for me, is using up leftovers that I have in the fridge (where I may have cooked extra just for the occasion), but there are certain foods that are really well suited to bento that you might want to start with. My picks are:

EGGS: Half a boiled egg or a couple of slices of Tamagoyaki (Rolled egg omelette, page 61) for colour and sustenance.

ANY PICKLES: Bright, fresh palate cleansers, they go well with anything, always.

ONIGIRI: The ultimate portable food (page 82).

OHITASHI: Any of the vegetable sides like the Okura ohitashi (page 126) or Cucumber and sesame salad (page 119) are perfect.

FRESH VEGETABLES OR FRUIT: Some cherry tomatoes or wedges of tomato, boiled corn cobs, wilted spinach, sliced apple, strawberries or grated carrot can add colour and freshness to a bento.

LEAVES: Use edible ones to separate different elements: lettuce, shiso leaf, or other herbs for aroma and colour, such as sansho or even basil.

POTATO SALAD: My ultimate favourite in a bento, as it goes with everything (page 203).

KARAAGE: Bite-sized pieces of Fried chicken (page 196) with a squirt of Japanese mayonnaise or some ponzu sauce over the top.

SATSUMAAGE: Serve Fried fish cakes (page 186) with a drizzle of soy sauce, a wedge of lemon and a side of daikon pickles.

KOROKKE: Croquettes (page 212) are perfect finger food, easy to eat; don't forget to drizzle some tonkatsu sauce (page 34) over the top.

BRAISED TOFU OR GYUDON: These saucy dishes (pages 138 or 103) are delicious in bento, as they flavour the rice too.

GRILLED FISH OR NANBANZUKE: Like breakfast, a piece of grilled salmon or mackerel go perfectly in a bento box too (pages 59 or 191).

KAWAII FOODS: My kids are big fans of frankfurter sausages cut to look like octopus (right down to black sesame eyes) and nori smiley faces on rice balls (made with a special hole-puncher-type thing that I bought at a daiso in Tokyo).

NON-JAPANESE FOODS: You don't need to pack a bento with only Japanese foods! Meatballs or kofta, pasta salad, grilled or roasted vegetables, hummus with vegetable sticks, bean salad, the choices are endless – just apply a similar method for choosing the foods and packing your ideal bento.

PACKING THE BENTO

Bento boxes often come with a built-in separator, which is handy if you want to keep hot foods away from fresh foods, or fruit for example, but you can also use leaves, as described on page 193, to separate different foods, or even paper, silicon or aluminium cupcake cases (mini ones are handy for sauces or pickles). Lay the rice down first (you can choose whether or not to separate a section of the box depending on what foods you are packing). On top of the rice, you can simply sprinkle furikake seasoning (page 31) or sesame seeds; otherwise, place proteins or vegetables on top of this. To the side you can pack things like potato salad, fresh fruit or vegetables, or things like corn cobs. Don't forget to slip in a pair of chopsticks or cutlery and a cloth napkin.

Pictured on the right is my aunt Yukiko's bento on a trip on the shinkansen (high speed train): onigiri made with barley and shinmai (new season rice, which is prized for being fresh, extremely moist and aromatic). Note that she keeps the nori separate so it stays crisp (you just wrap it around the rice when ready to eat). There are also containers with juicy nashi pear slices and her own homemade umeboshi (pickled plums). •

Fried Chicken

SERVES 4

か
ら
揚
げ

Karaage (pronounced 'kara-aghe') is said to have evolved from a Chinese method of cooking tofu in the 1920s. In fact, the *kara* of karaage means 'Tang Dynasty' and is used to describe things of Chinese origin. It is so popular today that you can find it in konbini (convenience stores), depachika (the food halls in the basements of department stores), as well as street food stalls and izakaya. When freshly fried, karaage is incredibly crisp on the outside and juicy inside, but they are also good cold, in a bento box. Like Tonkatsu (page 218), this goes really well with rice, a refreshing, crunchy cabbage salad like the one on page 132 and lemon wedges or ponzu sauce.

My good friend Yuta Mizoguchi is a talented chef from Oita (a city in Kyushu famous for their fried chicken, like toriten, tempura chicken and karaage, which is celebrated in an annual Karaage Festival), and he uses a little shortcut, where he simply mixes the marinade ingredients together with the starch into a batter and uses this to coat the chicken for a slightly different but just as delicious effect.

196

METHOD

You can leave the skin on the chicken, as it adds flavour and tenderness, but if you prefer not to, remove it, then cut into 4–5 cm (about 2 in) pieces – not too small, as these shrink when fried. Place in a container and coat the chicken with the ginger, soy sauce, sake and mirin. Leave to marinate for 15 minutes. I personally prefer karaage that is not too strongly flavoured, but you can leave it for longer if you do.

Sift the potato starch into a shallow bowl. Dip the marinated chicken pieces in it to coat entirely. Spread them out on a tray or wire rack as you go and let them 'dry out' slightly.

Pour enough vegetable oil for the chicken pieces to float into a small–medium saucepan (a depth of about 7 cm/2¾ in). Heat to 180°C (356°F) – a chopstick inserted into the oil should be immediately surrounded by energetic little bubbles when ready. Carefully lower the karaage into the oil in batches, filling the pan about halfway or two-thirds of the way, so you don't crowd the pan. Fry for 2–2½ minutes in total, or until deep golden brown. Lift out with a slotted spoon or with cooking chopsticks and transfer to a wire rack lined with kitchen paper.

INGREDIENTS

500 g (1 lb 2 oz) boneless
    chicken thighs
3 cm (1¼ in) piece of fresh root ginger,
    peeled and finely grated
2 teaspoons soy sauce
2 teaspoons sake
2 teaspoons mirin
    (or 1 teaspoon sugar)
100 g (generous ¾ cup) potato starch
vegetable oil, for frying

お気に入

メニュー

Sweet Soy Baked Chicken Wings

SERVES 4

手
羽
先
の
オ
ー
ブ
ン
焼
き

198

Growing up, this is one of the things we often made for parties with other Japanese-Australian families and it was always a hit with everyone, especially with the children – we nicknamed this dish 'yummy chicken', which says it all really.

The key here is marinating the chicken in the sauce. Don't be tempted to keep all the delicious marinade in the tray because it will just burn. Instead, drain off the marinade, cook it separately to reduce it, then use it as a glaze towards the end of cooking. You could use fish fillets here instead of the chicken, too. Sake is used for flavour and is a tenderiser, but if you don't have it, you can use a splash of white wine instead. If you don't have mirin handy, try a delicate honey instead, which is what my mother would have used.

METHOD

Separate the drumettes from the rest of the wing to have two pieces from each wing. You can trim the tips too, if you like, but I am all for the rather crunchy, almost burnt tip of the wing – no sense in wasting that.

Combine the rest of the ingredients in a ceramic baking dish and add the chicken, turning to coat well. Marinate in a cool place for at least 30 minutes (you can also do this well ahead of time, say in the morning before dinner or even the night before).

When you are ready to cook, preheat the oven to 200°C (400°F/gas 6).

Drain the marinade from the dish into a small saucepan and bring to a fast simmer for about 3–5 minutes, or until reduced slightly. Set aside.

Place the drained chicken wings in a greased baking dish large enough to fit them in one layer.

Bake for 30 minutes (or up to 15 minutes longer if you are using larger or meatier chicken wings), turning them over halfway through. They should be golden brown, bubbling and glistening. Brush the marinade-glaze over the wings and serve. If your family don't have problems with 'bits', this is lovely with some sesame seeds or green spring onion slices scattered over the top.

I don't believe there is any other way to eat chicken wings than with fingers. Serve with rice, any favourite sides (I like the Japanese Potato salad on page 203 and a cucumber salad or even a simple crunchy green salad), finger bowls with water for cleaning sticky fingers, and a separate bowl for collecting the bones.

INGREDIENTS

1 kg (2 lb 4 oz) chicken wings
2 garlic cloves, minced
3 cm (1¼ in) piece of fresh root ginger, peeled and finely grated
2 tablespoons mirin
80 ml (⅓ cup) soy sauce
1 tablespoon sake
1 tablespoon sesame oil
vegetable oil, for greasing
Steamed rice (page 80) and your favourite salads, to serve

TO GARNISH

toasted sesame seeds or the green part of spring onions (scallions), thinly sliced (optional)

お気に入

リメニュー

Miso Eggplant

SERVES 4 AS A SIDE DISH

な
す
田
楽

This is one of the first Japanese recipes I learned how to make when I moved to the US for university and was very far from home, and it is often still the dish I will make for someone unfamiliar with Japanese home cooking, because it is an instant winner – it has been my husband's favourite dish ever since I first made it for him. The silky eggplant (aubergine) together with the intensely flavourful, sweet miso sauce is just unforgettable. Dengaku sauce is commonly used to top tofu and other vegetables like daikon – the tofu is usually cut in a rectangle and skewered, then grilled. Personally, I also love this as a dip for crunchy cucumber sticks and if there is any sauce left over that's usually what I do with it.

You can eat nasu dengaku as a side dish, in which case this is enough for four to share, or turn it into a meal on its own with a crunchy, zingy cabbage salad (like the one on page 132) for two. In either case, you always need a bowl of freshly steamed rice nearby as a foil to the richness of this wonderful dish.

200

METHOD

Cut the eggplant in half lengthways, then score the flesh in a criss-cross pattern about 2 cm (¾ in) wide to make it easier to eat with chopsticks. I also like to trim a small (5 mm/¼ in) section of the skin on the bottom so that the eggplant doesn't wobble and sits flat.

Heat a 1–2 cm (½–¾ in) depth of vegetable oil in a frying pan (skillet) and fry the eggplant halves until they become deep brown and tender, about 3 minutes on each side. Frying is the secret to the silky texture. Remove carefully from the oil and let drain on a wire rack.

Heat the grill (broiler) element of your oven (or heat the oven to 220°C/ 430°F/gas 8 if you don't have this function).

Mix the miso, soy sauce, mirin and sugar together to a smooth paste and warm in a small saucepan to dissolve the sugar. If it is too thick, add a splash of water to loosen a little and mix until smooth, then remove from the heat.

Place the eggplants with the criss-cross sides up on a baking tray and cover with a thick coating of the miso mixture, about 1–2 tablespoons. Place under the grill (broiler) until the miso paste is bubbling around the edges, about 2–3 minutes (if using the oven to roast, place the tray on the top shelf and bake for several minutes or until the miso paste begins to bubble and brown slightly).

Serve sprinkled with toasted sesame seeds or finely chopped spring onions.

INGREDIENTS

1 large eggplant (aubergine)
vegetable oil, for frying
2 tablespoons brown miso
1 tablespoon soy sauce
1 tablespoon mirin
2 teaspoons sugar (I like raw demerara/
   turbinado sugar here)

TO GARNISH
sesame seeds or finely chopped spring
   onion (scallion) (green parts only)

お気に入

メニュー

お気に入

Potato Salad

SERVES 4

ポ
テ
ト
サ
ラ
ダ

203

METHOD

Place the cucumbers in a bowl with the salt and toss to combine. Let them sit for about 15 minutes, then rinse and squeeze out as much excess liquid as possible, then pat dry with kitchen paper.

Peel and roughly chop the potatoes and place them in a saucepan of cold water. Bring to the boil, then simmer for 15 minutes. Add the carrot and the onion for the last 5 minutes of cooking, then drain.

Place the potatoes, carrot and onion back into the saucepan and stir briefly – this will start breaking up the potatoes. You still want partial soft chunks of potato. Peel and mash the egg, then combine all the ingredients gently together along with some salt to taste.

INGREDIENTS

½ long Japanese cucumber, thinly sliced
½ teaspoon salt, plus extra to taste
3 large starchy potatoes (such as King Edward or Russet potatoes)
1 small carrot, peeled and thinly sliced
½ onion, thinly sliced lengthways
1 soft-boiled egg
2 tablespoons Japanese mayonnaise

NOTE

For softly set boiled eggs, simmer large, room-temperature eggs for 7 minutes. For firmer eggs, let them go for 10 minutes.

I love potato salad, but of all the potato salads in the world, I love Japanese potato salad the most. It is a Japanese version of a beloved dish in Italy, too, insalata russa (Russian salad), which was introduced to Japan after the Meiji Restoration. What I like so much about it, is that it is filled with plenty of other vegetables and that it is so creamy but not heavy, as Russian salad often is – in fact, this light, fluffy, 'creaminess' is achieved not by too much mayonnaise, but by using starchy potatoes rather than waxy potatoes. As you mix the boiled potatoes into the salad, they become partially mashed, a texture that is known as hoku hoku in Japanese.

THE WEST MEETS JAPAN

Always a rice lover.

Growing up as a half-Japanese, half-Western child, I embraced yoshoku food, as it was all instantly familiar; it was so… me – a mix of East and West.

洋

The word the Japanese use to describe their traditional cuisine is *washoku*, but the word *yoshoku* describes Western-style food. It dates back to the Meiji Restoration, a moment of upheaval politically, socially and gastronomically. The Japanese had been forced to reopen to the world after over two centuries of self-imposed isolation and the Emperor had announced the population was to embrace eating meat after avoiding it for over one thousand years (see page 16 for more on the 1,200-year-old meat ban). In order to help inspire them on how to prepare meat, cooks were encouraged to turn to Western dishes, which were reimagined to suit Japanese tastes.

After World War Two, these dishes became even more popular as foreign ingredients became easier to get. It was also a period of food shortages when rice was rationed, so wheat and bread (in particular American-style white sandwich bread) became a more important staple. Schools began offering milk and creamy milk-based dishes with milk powder supplied by the US to help boost children's nutrition after the war. The Japanese military and navy introduced many meat dishes to their meals, and department-store restaurants and 'family-style' diners started specialising in yoshoku. Many of these dishes not only became something unique, but are some of Japan's most beloved today and have become iconic Japanese classics in their own right – eaten with chopsticks alongside a bowl of rice, like washoku. It is, in fact, a form of Japanese cuisine.

Growing up as a half-Japanese, half-Western child, I embraced yoshoku food as it was all instantly familiar; it was so... me – a mix of East and West. Western ingredients and ideas – curry, corn, milk, crumbed cutlets, omelettes and sandwiches – but executed in a way that can only come about in a Japanese kitchen. I can honestly say that every single one of the recipes in this chapter is something that makes me so incredibly nostalgic for my childhood, and perhaps just as excited as when I was a child, too – because eating yoshoku is immensely fun, playful and comforting, as is cooking it, as there really are no rules. ●

207

Me with my parents.

洋

Fried Rice Omelette

オ
ム
ラ
イ
ス

There is something about egg, rice and tomatoes that will always be a winning combination for me and it probably has something to do with the fact that this is such a comforting dish and one that is often made for children (but enjoyed by everybody). In this case, the tomato comes from tomato ketchup and it just works. It cannot be substituted, no matter how much you might turn your nose up at the idea.

Don't be intimidated by omuraisu – it is a very simple, quick dish, like fried rice, that just happens to have an omelette sitting on top of it. The key is not to overcook the omelette, so that it remains slightly soft and custardy and, rather importantly, very pale – not browned. You don't have to do the cheffy, wobbly omelette that was made popular in the 1980s film *Tampopo*, where a boy and a homeless man break into a restaurant and cook the most beautiful omuraisu you'll ever see: softly scrambled egg omelette that is placed on top of a mound of ketchup rice and sliced across its length, spilling out dramatically over the rice. It's a fantastic scene. But this one is a little simpler and more achievable.

METHOD

Mix together the tomato passata or paste, ketchup and soy sauce, and set aside.

Heat half of the oil in a frying pan (skillet) or wok over a low–medium heat and gently cook the onion and carrot with a pinch of salt, stirring occasionally, until just cooked through, but not browning, about 5–7 minutes. Add the chicken and continue cooking until cooked through, about 3 minutes.

Tip in the rice and break it up if it is in clumps. Once the rice is well incorporated, add the sauce and toss, cooking for a further 2–3 minutes, or until the rice is coated evenly. Set aside and keep warm. (I like to use two rice bowls to shape the ketchup rice; I fill the bowls, turn them upside down on the serving plates and leave the bowls on to keep the rice warm while I cook the omelettes.)

For the omelette, clean out the pan. Beat the eggs together with the water and a good pinch of salt. Heat the pan over a high heat and grease with the rest of the oil. Pour in half of the egg mixture to cover the pan like a crêpe. This next part is fast – no more than 1 minute of cooking. Quickly but briefly scramble the eggs, then leave so the bottom sets but on top the surface is still wobbly and a bit custardy. Flip the top third over, then the bottom third over and remove from the heat. Remove the bowl from the top of one ketchup rice, place the omelette on top and serve.

Repeat with the second omelette and serve immediately.

VARIATIONS

You can use ham, bacon or pre-cooked chicken (if you happen to have some, this is a great way to use leftover roast or poached chicken). Or you can leave the chicken out if you don't have it or want a vegetarian version – try instead some chopped mushrooms, peas or the addition of spring onions (scallions).

209

INGREDIENTS

1 tablespoon tomato passata
   or tomato paste (concentrated puree)
1 tablespoon tomato ketchup, plus extra
   to garnish
1 tablespoon soy sauce
1 tablespoon vegetable oil
1 small onion, finely chopped
½ carrot, peeled and finely chopped
salt
100 g (3½ oz) chicken, diced into
   1 cm (½ in) cubes
1 cup cooked, cold Japanese short-grain
   rice (day-old is fine)
3 eggs
1 tablespoon water

食

Creamy Corn Soup

SERVES 4

コ
ー
ン
ポ
タ
ー
ジ
ュ

To an outsider, this may seem like an odd one to find in a Japanese cookbook, but if you grew up as a child in Japan, you would be very familiar with corn soup or corn potage (which is pronounced 'kon-potaju'), as it is known in Japan. It's something often on the children's menu in restaurants and is so accessible — it's sold everywhere you can imagine: as instant soup, in konbini, even in vending machines on train-station platforms, alongside cans of coffee and bottles of oolong tea – cold or even warm! But it is incredibly easy to make at home – you only need two ingredients, four if you count salt and water. It's a soup that can get you through the hot, humid summers (when corn is at its best) when chilled, where it thickens, turning almost into a delicious silky pudding. When autumn (fall) comes around and you need a warm version, then you have a deeply comforting, heavily nostalgic soup. It freezes well, too.

I like to use fresh corn for this incredibly simple recipe because boiling the whole corn cob infuses the water – it becomes a delicious corn stock. Then you only need milk to turn it into a rich and satisfying soup (some like to use cream, but I find that version a bit heavy).

210

METHOD

Place the corn in a large saucepan, cover with the water and add the salt. Simmer for 20 minutes over a low–medium heat. Remove the corn cobs, saving the corn stock. When cool enough to handle, cut off the corn kernels.

Blend the kernels with about 500 ml (2 cups) of the corn stock, or more if you prefer it more brothy. Pass this through a fine-mesh sieve to remove some of the tougher fibres, so you are left with a very smooth corn puree.

Place the corn puree back in the saucepan, add the milk and bring it to a very gentle simmer over a low heat. You must be careful that it doesn't burn or overflow, as milk has a tendency to do, so stir it gently and keep checking on it. Try not to scrape the bottom of the pot in case it has formed a film. It's better to let this film protect the rest of the soup than break it up and have little brown bits floating in the soup. It only needs about 5 minutes of this gentle heating to thicken to perfection. Remove from the heat and enjoy right away, or serve it chilled. If you like, garnish with chives.

VARIATION

If you are lactose intolerant or vegan, try this with soy or another plant-based milk.

INGREDIENTS

4 whole, fresh corn cobs
1.5 litres (6 cups) water
1 teaspoon salt
500 ml (2 cups) milk
finely chopped chives, to garnish (optional)

洋

食

Curry Croquettes

MAKES 8

カ
レ
ー
コ
ロ
ッ
ケ

Korokke are nothing more than croquettes that date to around the same time as tonkatsu, the late 1800s, and these are another favourite with children, perfect for putting in bento boxes or for a simple snack with Tonkatsu sauce (page 34) or turned into a sando. These are flavoured with Japanese curry, because (as you'll read more about on page 216) it is a national obsession. Among the curry-flavoured delights on offer that I love, you can find karepan (Japanese curry-filled dough balls that are crumbed and fried), curry noodles (udon, ramen or soba, you name it, in a brothy version of Japanese curry), there's even yaki curry (a baked rice gratin, like a cross between Curry rice, page 216, and Doria, page 226). It doesn't take much to insert your favourite Japanese curry into a dish.

洋

METHOD

Peel the potatoes and roughly chop. Place in a saucepan of cold water and bring to the boil, covered. Simmer for 15 minutes, or until soft, then drain and mash roughly with a fork – you should leave some chunky bits for texture. Let cool completely.

Heat the oil in a frying pan (skillet) over a medium heat and cook the onion and carrot with a good pinch of salt, stirring often, until the vegetables begin to soften, about 4 minutes. Add the minced meat and continue stirring until the meat breaks up and is cooked, a further 4 minutes or so. Add the curry and a tablespoon or so of water to help distribute it evenly, particularly if using a curry cube. It shouldn't be saucy, but just enough to help the cube dissolve. Taste and add salt, if needed.

Add the mixture to the cooled potatoes and stir through well. Let the mixture cool completely, then shape into 8 oval patties, about 70 g (2½ oz) each. Pat them well so they are compact and there are no air pockets inside.

Prepare three shallow bowls, each filled with the flour, egg and panko, respectively. Dust the patties first completely in flour, then dip in the egg to coat evenly and finally into the panko crumbs, ensuring there are no spots missing. Let rest on a tray or a plate to dry out a little before frying, even 10 minutes is helpful for a good crisp coating. If you want to prepare this ahead of time, at this stage the korokke can be kept in the fridge, uncovered, for several hours until you are ready to fry.

Fill a heavy-based pan (I like a cast-iron frying pan/skillet) with a 2 cm (¾ in) depth of vegetable oil and heat to 180°C (356°F) – a chopstick inserted in the oil should immediately be surrounded by vigorous little bubbles. Fry the korokke a few at a time for 2 minutes in total, flipping them over halfway to ensure an even golden brown colouring. Transfer to a wire rack lined with absorbent kitchen paper while you fry the rest.

These are delicious warm or cold.

VARIATIONS

You could also replace the meat with prawns (shrimp) or minced (ground) chicken. Vegetarians have so many options with other vegetables – some good ones to try are sauteed mushrooms, cooked peas, corn, kabocha pumpkin or chestnuts.

213

INGREDIENTS

3 starchy potatoes (King Edwards or Russets, for example) (roughly 500 g/1 lb 2 oz)
1 tablespoon vegetable oil, plus extra for frying
¼ onion, finely chopped
¼ carrot, peeled and finely chopped
a pinch of salt, or as needed
200 g (7 oz) minced (ground) pork or beef
1 cube of Japanese instant curry (or 2 teaspoons curry powder or garam marsala)
2 tablespoons plain (all-purpose) flour
1 egg, beaten
40 g (½ cup) Panko breadcrumbs (page 33), crushed a little to make them a bit finer

食

洋

'If you visit a hundred homes
in Japan, you'll find a hundred
styles of curry.'

TADASHI ONO AND
HARRIS SALAT IN
*JAPANESE SOUL
COOKING*

食

Curry Rice

SERVES 4

カ
レ
ー
ラ
イ
ス

216

This has been on regular rotation at my house since I was a child, and it still is; my father, Ian, makes this once a week now that my mother has taught him how to make Japanese curry (*kare raisu* in Japanese).

Japanese curry is unlike any 'curry' you might know from South Asian countries and that is partly because of the nature of yoshoku cuisine but also because this recipe did a roundabout route to get to Japan. Curry arrived in Japan via the British Royal Navy during the Meiji Restoration, a period when India was under British colonial rule. It arrived in the form of British 'C&B' curry powder, so it was considered Western food, not Indian. The first kare raisu recipe appeared in a Japanese cookbook in 1872, and shortly afterwards in a restaurant in Tokyo. Curry became a staple in the Japanese naval and army kitchens at the turn of the century and this in turn brought curry into homes and even into school lunches. Today, the Japanese Navy still serves curry every Friday (like my dad) and it is considered a national dish.

One of the first things that happened during the birth of Japanese curry was that the broth needed to be thick enough so that it could be easily eaten with rice (with the help of a spoon). This can be achieved with a French-style roux base of butter, flour and liquid, or it can be thickened in a more Japanese style using a potato starchy slurry right at the end of cooking, which is my preference. Then there is the spice mix. Today, Japanese S&B curry powder is one of the best known and has been for a century. It contains a mix of 17 spices, such as turmeric, coriander, fenugreek, cumin, cinnamon, fennel, ginger and star anise, to name a few. But there are as many different recipes for Japanese curry as there are cooks who make it, not to mention regional versions from venison curry in Hokkaido to oyster curry in Hiroshima and bitter melon curry in Okinawa, so feel free to make this your own too. The Japanese Navy version even has Cheddar cheese in it.

In Japanese homes, it is most often made with a packet mix in the form of waxy cubes that you just add to a stew of meat and vegetables (most often a homely combination of beef or pork, carrot, onion and potato). The cubes dissolve, instantly turning the stew into a thick, fragrant, mild Japanese curry. Everyone has their favourite brand (or perhaps two favourite brands mixed together) that they pump up with 'secret' ingredients to make theirs unique – honey, grated nashi pear or prunes for sweetness, or coffee for colour and balance. My mother told me of a friend who liked to add dark chocolate to hers. I knew instantly how well that works as a flavour in a meaty stew – chocolate or cocoa is a popular addition to an age-old Tuscan wild boar stew that I love. But when you make curry from scratch, it is already unique, and trust me, even better than any instant curries.

洋

METHOD

Chop the meat into 3 cm (1¼ in) cubes. Heat a little vegetable oil in a heavy-based saucepan over a high heat and sear the meat on all sides, about 4–5 minutes in total. Remove the meat and set aside.

Reduce the heat to medium and add the butter to the pan, followed by the onion and ginger, and stir quickly so the onion doesn't burn, cooking with all the browned bits gathering at the bottom of the pan, for about 2–3 minutes. Deglaze the pan with the mirin and scrape the brown goodness off the bottom as it bubbles. Add the spices, toss to coat everything in them, then add the dashi, soy sauce, salt, vegetables and meat. Cover and cook for 20 minutes, turning the heat down to a gentle simmer.

Meanwhile, make a little slurry with the potato starch and water.

After the simmering time, add the chocolate to the curry, stir though, then immediately add the slurry. Let it all bubble for 1 or maybe 2 more minutes, or until thickened. Serve immediately, ladled over warm rice. Put some pickles on the side as a garnish – I love Beni shoga (red pickled ginger, page 36) and rakkyo pickles (pickled Chinese onion).

INGREDIENTS

300 g (10½ oz) pork loin (or beef, or other protein of choice)
vegetable oil, for greasing
40 g (1½ oz) butter
1 onion, sliced
4 cm (1½ in) piece of fresh root ginger, peeled and finely grated
2 tablespoons mirin (or white wine)
1 tablespoon curry powder
2 teaspoons garam marsala
¼ teaspoon chilli powder (optional)
500 ml (2 cups) Dashi (page 30), chicken stock or water
1 tablespoon soy sauce
½ teaspoon salt
1 carrot, peeled and chopped into chunky slices
200 g (7 oz) potato, peeled and chopped
80 g (2¾ oz) mushrooms, chopped roughly
2 teaspoons potato starch (or cornflour/corn starch)
1 tablespoon water, or as needed
1 cube (about 10 g/¼ oz) of dark chocolate, minimum 70% cocoa solids

TO SERVE
cooked rice
pickles of choice

食

Fried Pork Cutlet with Miso Sauce

SERVES 4

味
噌
カ
ツ

INGREDIENTS

MISO SAUCE
1 garlic clove, finely grated
3 cm (1¼ in) piece of fresh root ginger, peeled and finely grated
75 g (¼ cup) hatcho miso (see note)
2 tablespoons mirin
1 tablespoon sake
2 tablespoons sugar

TONKATSU
40 g (⅓ cup) plain (all-purpose) flour
2 eggs, beaten
80 g (1 cup) Panko breadcrumbs (page 33)
4 × 150 g (5½ oz) slices of pork loin, about 2 cm (¾ in) thick
vegetable oil, for frying

TO SERVE
300 g (10½ oz) cabbage, finely shredded (see note)
a handful of cherry tomatoes
Steamed rice (page 80)
Miso soup (page 54, optional)

NOTES
Hatcho miso is a pure soybean, darker and less sweet miso – it has a truly punchy flavour. Use red miso or brown miso if you can't find it.

For ultra-crunchy cabbage, after shredding, place in a bowl of ice-cold water until needed. Dry with a salad spinner or on clean dish towels before serving.

A thick pork cutlet, coated in crisp panko crumbs, fried and served with a specially made sauce, tonkatsu is iconic among the best-known Japanese dishes. It was invented over a century ago at Rengatei, a restaurant in Tokyo's Ginza neighbourhood, by chef Motojiro Kida, who was inspired by the Milanese veal cotoletta, and served it on rice with finely sliced raw cabbage – still the classic way to enjoy it today. But it's so loved, there are countless other ways to find tonkatsu: katsu-sando, sandwiched between fluffy shokupan bread like the Ebi furai sando (page 223), or katsudon, a rice bowl where the cutlet is cooked with a beaten egg over the top of it like the Gyudon (page 103 – an excellent way to use leftover tonkatsu, if that is ever a thing) or katsu curry, where the pork is served under a blanket of Japanese curry (page 216).

One family trip to Tokyo, we stumbled across a tonkatsu restaurant in Ginza called Misokatsu Yabaton and it was so good we went back multiple times. The prized pork comes from southern Kyushu and even the breadcrumbs are specially made. But what they are best known for, which the name gives away, is a specialty from Nagoya – between Tokyo and Osaka – where they load a miso-rich sauce rather than the usual Worcestershire sauce–based tonkatsu sauce onto their juicy pork cutlets: misokatsu. It is, to put it plainly, out of this world.

METHOD
To make the sauce, place the ingredients in a small pan and gently warm over a low heat, stirring to help the sugar dissolve. You may like to add a splash of water if it is too thick, as this sauce should be pouring consistency. Take off the heat when it begins to bubble or when the desired consistency is reached.

For the tonkatsu, prepare three shallow bowls, each filled with the flour, eggs and panko respectively. Dust the pieces of pork first completely in flour, then dip into the egg to coat evenly and finally into the panko crumbs, ensuring there are no spots missing. Let rest on a tray or a plate to dry out a little before frying, even 10 minutes is helpful for a good crisp coating. If you want to prepare ahead, at this stage the tonkatsu can be kept in the fridge, uncovered, for several hours.

Fill a heavy-based pan (I like cast iron) with a 2 cm (¾ in) depth of vegetable oil and heat to 180°C (356°F) – a chopstick inserted should immediately be surrounded by vigorous little bubbles. Fry the tonkatsu (you may only be able to fit two at a time) for 3 minutes on each side. Transfer to a wire rack lined with absorbent kitchen paper while you fry the rest.

Arrange the cabbage and tomatoes on one side of your plates. Slice the tonkatsu into 1.5 cm (½ in) strips and place each cutlet on the plates. Pour over the sauce (keep any extra in a jug on the table for people to help themselves) and serve with rice (and, if you want a complete experience, a bowl of miso soup, too).

洋

食

洋

Shokupan was our breakfast on the odd occasion that Obaachan didn't make her usual breakfast. My grandfather would grill the oversized, thick slices of bread – if it was winter, it might even be grilled right over the gas heater – and slather it with butter and honey. I can still taste it when I think about it today. Shokupan is simply an everyday, pillowy soft white bread that is much bigger than the standard sandwich loaves found in Western countries. It is also sold in whole loaves – not pre-cut – so rather than thin sandwich bread slices, it is usually cut at home as you need it in very thick slices (it is much easier to cut thick slices from a soft loaf than thin ones by hand).

To satisfy my nostalgic cravings I had no choice but to make it myself, and in my research on this recipe, I found Shihoko Ura, who pens the Japanese food blog *Chopstick Chronicles* from Tasmania, has the most thorough and well-explained shokupan recipe that I've tried. This very recipe's bones are inspired by hers, so if you need a video for more guidance, I would recommend the one on her video channel too.

Yudane (湯種) is a Japanese bread-making method and tangzhong (borrowing the Japanese word with Chinese pronunciation of the same characters 湯種) was invented as a modified version of yudane by Taiwanese pastry chef Yvonne Chen in 2007, who described it as the Japanese 'secret ingredient' to soft, pillowy bread. In both methods a portion of flour and water are partially cooked and added to the dough. With yudane you simply mix the flour with just-boiled water and let it rest for several hours, whereas tangzhong is made by cooking the flour and water together over heat, resulting in a starchy gel. In both cases the hot water causes the starch to gelatinise (the bread is able to hold onto water better and for longer, keeping it from drying out) and this is what makes the bread so soft and sweet, and keeps it soft for days. Yudane helps to add strength to the bread and creates a high rise, perfect for shokupan, and gives it an almost brioche-like texture. For best results, make the yudane the night before and keep it in the fridge.

METHOD

For the yudane, mix the flour and boiling hot water in a small bowl until combined. You should have a rather thick, sticky dough. Cover and let rest overnight in the fridge, but if you're in a hurry, leave it to rest for at least 1 hour, or even better 4 hours – the longer the better.

When the yudane is ready, in a large bowl, combine the strong and plain flours, along with the salt. In a jug or bowl (or in the pan where you have warmed the milk), whisk together the yeast and sugar with the warm milk until the sugar is dissolved. Pour this mixture into the flour and combine until you have a shaggy dough. Cover and leave to rest for 10–15 minutes. If the dough ever feels too wet or sticky, a rest like this will help.

Cont. >

Japanese Milk Bread

MAKES 2 SMALL SQUARE LOAVES

食
パ
ン

221

INGREDIENTS

YUDANE
50 g (⅓ cup) strong white bread flour (such as manitoba or other high-protein flour – see notes overleaf)
50 ml (scant ¼ cup) just-boiled water

DOUGH
120 g (generous ¾ cup) strong white bread flour (see notes on following page)
150 g (1 cup) plain (all-purpose) flour
½ teaspoon salt
3 g (⅛ oz/1¼ teaspoons) dried active yeast or 12 g (½ oz) fresh yeast
2 tablespoons sugar
160 ml (⅔ cup) milk, warmed to body temperature
50 g (1¾ oz) unsalted butter, diced and left to soften
vegetable oil, for greasing

Strong white bread flour, such as manitoba or other flours that have a protein content greater than 12% protein, is used to help make the dough more elastic and give the bread lift. Plain flour alone won't give you the lift you need for this soft, fluffy bread.

While traditional shokupan is very large and square, it is difficult to find the correct pans outside of Japan, so the recipe here is perfect for the smaller European-style pullman loaf tins. I particularly like a small, square 10 cm (4 in) bread pan for 250 g (9 oz) of dough and I leave the lid off. This is enough to make two loaves in two separate square pans, or one longer one in a 10 cm × 20 cm (4 in × 8 in) pan.

Upon hearing I wanted to take on shokupan as I was testing recipes, my wonderful baker friend Laura Lazzaroni, said to me: 'You have a mixer, right? You won't be able to make milk bread without one.' Well, I still don't have a mixer. I make this by hand. Yes, it is a little hard work, but it can be done – like hand-made udon or pasta, you just need a little elbow grease. I actually look forward to my kneading sessions, it is the perfect mindful activity to de-stress, better than a punching bag. Put on your favourite music and just go for it! The key is taking little intervals to rest (for you and the dough, but especially for the dough) if you need to. You could of course do it with less effort in a mixer, but even with a mixer you need to make sure the dough is being kneaded more vigorously than regular bread doughs. Don't let this put you off, the result is so satisfying and at the first inhale of the buttery, sweet bread aroma, you will be so glad you made this.

Add the yudane and butter to the dough and knead until well combined. Keep kneading. Resist trying to add flour if you're kneading by hand. It will be sticky at first, but as you knead it will come together beautifully. Some like to do the 'slap and fold' method, where you slap the sticky dough down onto the work surface, fold over, then slap again. I do this by hand in a large, wide ceramic bowl that is heavy so it stays still, but you could do this on a work surface if you prefer. I also like to knead in a cross shape, where you use both hands, alternately, first pushing the dough from left to right, diagonally, then from right to left, diagonally as if drawing an 'X'.

Do this at your own pace if you are doing this by hand, it should take roughly 20–25 minutes; 10 minutes in a mixer. If you are using a mixer, use a rather vigorous setting and in both cases knead until the dough suddenly starts to pull away from the sides of the bowl or from your hands rather than sticking to your hands. It should come together into a beautifully soft, smooth ball.

Leave to rest for 10–15 minutes. At this point, a good test that the gluten is well developed is the 'window pane' test. Take a little ball of dough and stretch it between your hands. Hold it up to the window – you should be able to stretch it thin enough that you can detect light through the dough without it breaking. Keep kneading if not. When it reaches this stage, place it in a large, lightly oiled bowl, cover and let it rise until doubled in size, at least 1–2 hours at room temperature (more if it's a cold day; less if it's hot).

To shape the shokupan, tip the dough out onto a clean work surface. Divide the dough into two equal parts and keep one covered. Roll or slightly flatten the first piece of dough into a rectangle. Fold like you would a business letter, down one third from the top, then fold in the other third from the bottom. Next, roll it up (not too tightly) from the short side. It should be compact, not quite a ball though, so now roll it gently into a nice ball with a taut top by cupping your hand over the top and rolling while pulling it towards you, turning, and pulling it towards you and so on, until you have a nice ball that holds its shape – the seam should stay on the bottom.

If you are baking in two separate square tins, place in an oiled tin and cover with a dish towel, then repeat the process with the other half of the dough. If making one longer loaf, place the two dough balls side by side in the oiled tin. Let the dough rise until it reaches the top of the pan – this could take 2 hours, depending on the temperature of the room. What is important is to have patience and just wait for it to rise completely. If you put it in the oven before it reaches the top of the pan, it won't have the lovely lift it should have.

When you are ready to bake, heat the oven to 180°C (350°F/gas 4).

Spray the top of the bread loaves with some water (if you don't have a spray bottle, just flick some water lightly with wet hands) and bake for 20 minutes, or until the top is deep golden brown, risen and puffed. Let cool completely before slicing (if you can resist) into extra thick slices. Any uneaten bread can stay soft for several days in an airtight container.

洋

Fried Prawn Sandwiches

SERVES 2

エビフライサンド

This is a highly nostalgic dish for me. I was a young teenager. My stylish grandfather, Chodo (who didn't like the idea of ageing and insisted his grandchildren call him *Otosan* – 'father'), took me on one of his food shopping trips to Mitsukoshi department-store in Tokyo.

A Buddhist priest, I was used to seeing my grandfather in his long pale grey and white flowing robes and perfectly white tabi socks around the temple, but when he went out to Tokyo, he would change into smart casual clothes, wearing a beret to cover his bald head, a pair of sunglasses and carrying a cool leather bag. He excelled in Kendo, one of the Japanese martial arts practised with a bamboo sword, and he was a talented painter and calligrapher – the smell of ink still reminds me of him – and a passionate photographer with a collection of wonderful cameras. He would often have his Polaroid camera within arm's reach to capture everyday moments of us children. He took beautiful black and white photographs of my mother as a child. When I look at them I can spot his photographer's eye instantly.

I followed him around Mitsukoshi while he bought his favourite foods in the basement food hall – satsumaage fish cakes, his favourite furikake (see page 31) and manju (sweet red bean cakes). I still love wandering into a depachika (the name for these department-store food halls) and taking in all the sights and smells, inevitably giving in to some tastes, too. Ebi furai sando are nothing more than fluffy shokupan sandwiches filled with prawns (shrimp) crumbed in panko and fried, Japanese mayonnaise and tonkatsu sauce. They are popular in a bento box for taking on the shinkansen (bullet train) and you can also find them in a modern-style cafe on the top floors of department stores, where we stopped for a bite to eat after shopping. I can remember thinking, 'this is the best thing I've ever eaten'.

223

Cont. >

My grandfather.

224

INGREDIENTS

EBI FURAI
6 extra-large raw prawns
    (jumbo shrimp)
35 g (¼ cup) plain (all-purpose) flour
1 egg, beaten
40 g (½ cup) Panko breadcrumbs
    (page 33)
vegetable oil, for frying
salt

SANDO
finely shredded cabbage
4 thick slices of fluffy white bread,
    such as Shokupan (page 221)
Japanese mayonnaise (optional)
Tonkatsu sauce (page 34) (optional)
shichimi togarashi or chilli
    powder (optional)
a squeeze of lemon or lemon wedges

METHOD

Carefully remove the heads and shells of the prawns but leave the tails on. Remove the dark digestive tract with a skewer or a toothpick, pulling it out rather than cutting down the spine. You can help keep their shapes by making some small incisions along the belly side so they won't curl up when cooking.

Prepare three shallow bowls, each filled with the flour, egg and panko respectively. Dust the prawns first completely in flour, then dip in the egg to coat evenly, then back into the flour and back into the egg for a double coating, then finally into the panko crumbs, ensuring there are no spots missing. Let rest on a tray or a plate to dry out a little before frying, even 10 minutes is helpful for a good crisp coating. If you want to prepare this ahead of time, at this stage the prawns can be kept in the fridge, uncovered, for several hours until ready to fry.

Fill a heavy-based saucepan (I like cast iron and something not too big) with a 2.5 cm (1 in) depth of vegetable oil and heat to 180°C (356°F) – a chopstick inserted in the oil should immediately be surrounded by vigorous little bubbles. Fry the prawns for 2 minutes in total, turning periodically until they are evenly deep golden brown. Transfer to a wire rack lined with absorbent kitchen paper and sprinkle generously with salt.

To make the sandwiches, simply place a tuft of shredded cabbage on one side of the bread, lay three prawns on top, with their tails sticking out slightly. Squirt over some Japanese mayonnaise, some tonkatsu sauce, a sprinkle of shichimi togarashi or chilli powder, if you like, and even a squeeze of lemon (or serve with lemon wedges for squeezing over as you like). Lay another piece of bread on top and then cut into two rectangles. Repeat for the other sandwich. Crusts on or off, your choice.

洋

食

Seafood Rice Gratin

SERVES 4

ド
リ
ア

This is another dish I remember having for the first time with my aunt, Yukiko, at one of the cafes at the top of the fashionable Mitsukoshi department store. One forkful of the rich, creamy seafood and rice gratin and I was hooked. This yoshoku dish has an interesting origin story, too. It's named after Andrea Doria, a 15th-century admiral and condottiero from Genova, but no one is sure why – perhaps because he was considered one of the most important naval leaders of his day and so had a connection with the sea. In *Japanese Soul Cooking*, Tadashi Ono and Harris Salat credit a Swiss chef in Yokohama for inventing doria when a customer asked for something comforting. I would say the chef nailed it.

METHOD

Remove the heads, tails and shells of the prawns and set these aside in a saucepan. Remove and discard the digestive tract of the prawns with a sharp knife and set aside the prawns somewhere cool until needed.

Heat the butter in a saucepan over a low–medium heat, and cook the onion with a pinch of salt, stirring gently. When it begins to turn translucent, after 3–4 minutes, add the mushrooms and cook until tender, a further 2–3 minutes. Increase the heat to medium, add the prawns and scallops, along with another pinch of salt and the wine, and cook for 1 minute. Add the rice and toss to break it up and combine well. When it is warmed through and clump-free, about 1 minute, remove from the heat.

Divide the rice among four individual ovenproof dishes (or place in one large casserole dish or Dutch oven).

Make the bechamel by adding milk to the reserved prawn shells. Slowly heat until the milk is very hot, but turn it off just before it boils. It will look a little curdled, but don't worry, this is a normal reaction, it won't affect the texture of the bechamel. Strain to remove the prawn shells.

In a small saucepan, melt the butter over a low–medium heat, then whisk in the flour and continue stirring, letting the flour cook for a minute or so. Add the prawn-infused milk a little at a time to avoid lumps, stirring continuously until the bechamel is smooth and thickened. Add the salt, then stir the bechamel evenly through the rice. Scatter the Parmesan over the top.

Just before you are ready to serve, heat the oven to 250°C (475°F) or turn on the grill (broil) function of your oven if you have it. Place the dishes on the top shelf of your oven and bake or grill for 5–7 minutes, or until the top is bubbling with golden brown patches.

INGREDIENTS

300 g (10½ oz) raw prawns (shrimp)
1 tablespoon butter
1 onion, finely chopped
2 pinches of salt
100 g (3½ oz) mushrooms, chopped
240 g (8½ oz) scallops, about 8
60 ml (¼ cup) white wine (or sake)
3 cups cold cooked rice
35 g (⅓ cup) grated Parmesan cheese

BECHAMEL
750 ml (3 cups) milk
50 g (1¾ oz) butter
35 g (¼ cup) plain (all-purpose) flour
¼ teaspoon salt (or to taste)

洋

食

AMAIMONO

甘
い
物

SWEETS

甘

Dessert in a Japanese meal is more often than not a piece of fresh fruit. I can remember almost every seasonal visit to my grandparents based on the fruit we had at the end of a meal, each one so memorable and a benchmark for every piece of fruit I ever ate after that, because of the quality and flavour you get from eating fruit in the height of seasonality, as is so appreciated in Japan (read more about shun, the peak of seasonality, on page 113 – it is really what makes Japanese produce so special). Fragrant strawberries in spring, the juiciest blushing pink peaches that you could smell from the stairs leading to the house in the summer, perfectly round purple grapes, juicy nashi pears and red Fuji apples almost as big as my head in early autumn (fall), heavy persimmons from the tree in the garden, picked and left to blet on the frosty windowsill until completely jammy inside, and mountains of mandarins in the winter. This was our dessert.

But traditional Japanese sweets are aplenty. They're called wagashi and they were designed to be enjoyed with a cup of bitter matcha during a tea ceremony, to balance the bitterness of the intense green tea with their sweetness, and to catch your eye with their pretty, seasonal designs.

All my favourite Japanese sweets are ones with Anko (adzuki bean paste, page 234) – sweet, dark and either chunky or smooth, with a texture rather like sweet chestnut puree. You can find it as a filling in Dorayaki pancakes (page 247), mochi (soft and delicate rice flour balls), inside yeasted buns, made into jelly (yokan) or topping shaved ice in the summer (kakigori), even served as a sweet, warming soup in the winter (Zenzai, page 240). I also adore an old-fashioned Anmitsu (page 238), a melange of Japanese specialties in one bowl – some cubes of kanten jelly, soft rice dango balls, a blob of anko and perhaps some ice cream, all with a drizzle of dark sugar syrup. I love nothing more than finding a traditional tea house in the middle of busy Tokyo to stop and have a refreshing treat like this in the middle of the afternoon.

Growing up, I loved every kind of mochi; my grandfather had a soft spot for them, too. He would travel to a century-old wagashi shop near Ueno in Tokyo called Tsuruse just to buy his favourite mochi, which also became my favourites. One is called fumanju, where a perfectly smooth koshian anko filling hides inside mochi dough made of wheat gluten, flavoured and coloured with Japanese yomogi (mugwort or artemisia, the wild herb that is used for making absinthe and vermouth). It is a highly seasonal specialty that you can find in the summertime, so it is kept very fresh and chilled, wrapped in a bamboo leaf, making these so appealing on a humid summer's day. The other is mame daifuku, which is basically like the classic mochi in the recipe on page 243 before you add a strawberry, but the mochi dough has whole adzuki beans in the dough as well, giving the mochi a polka-dot appearance – these are Tsuruse's specialty.

There are also many Western sweets that have made their way into Japanese cuisine and been tinkered with to suit Japanese tastes (known as yogashi, like the yoshoku dishes in the previous chapter), with beloved flavours like hojicha (roasted green tea), matcha (powdered green tea) and kinako (roasted soybean powder). Kasutera (the Japanese pronunciation of 'castella') is a classic example – a Portuguese madeira-like cake brought to Japan in the 16th century – while soft and fluffy cakes like chiffon cake, sponge rolls and pound cakes are also very popular. ●

231

'Bean paste is the soul of dorayaki.'

—

TOKUE, FROM THE NOVEL
SWEET BEAN PASTE
BY DURIAN SUKEGAWA

Hojicha Ice Cream

SERVES 6

ほうじ茶アイスクリーム

The easiest no-churn ice cream hack ever is whipped cream and sweetened condensed milk. You can add any flavours really to this simple preparation, but hojicha ice cream is my weakness.

Hojicha has a gentle, toasted, nutty flavour. It is a green tea, but it isn't bitter, it is roasted in a porcelain pot over charcoal, which is what contributes to those toasty notes. It's delicious as iced tea in the summer and comforting as hot tea in the winter. The roasting also removes the amount of caffeine in the tea, so hojicha is even enjoyed by children before going to sleep. Here, I like to make a cold infusion of the tea leaves with the cream for a perfectly balanced flavour. If you can't get the tea leaves, you can try with powdered tea – it may be a stronger flavour, so use less, and you won't need to wait for the infusion either.

232

INGREDIENTS

4 tablespoons hojicha tea leaves
500 ml (2 cups) single (whipping) cream
160 ml (⅔ cup) sweetened
  condensed milk
hojicha powder or extra hojicha tea
  leaves, to serve

METHOD

Mix the hojicha and cream together, giving it a little stir to combine (I just like to put the tea directly into the carton of cream for less washing up). Leave to infuse for 8 hours or overnight in the fridge.

Strain (if using leaves) and then whip until peaks hold. Fold through the sweetened condensed milk, then transfer to a freezer-proof container and freeze for 6–8 hours. This is best enjoyed not long after it is made, but it will keep well for a couple of weeks.

Serve with a little dusting of hojicha powder or just some hojicha tea leaves over the top.

甘

い物

Adzuki Bean Paste

MAKES ABOUT 750 G (2½ CUPS)

餡
子

I would substitute all the chocolate in the world for anko. I love it in all its forms and offerings, which are as numerous as the uses for chocolate. You'll notice it appears often in this chapter; hidden inside tender mochi with a whole strawberry, inside soft, fluffy buns or in a warming sweet soup. It's even delicious spread over buttered shokupan toast served with a mug of unsweetened green tea – the bitterness of matcha balances out the sweetness of anko so perfectly.

An, which is simply the preparation of sweet, starchy pulses, can be found also in the form of shiroan, made from a type of white kidney bean, kurian (chestnut paste, page 247) and even sweet potato. Anko has two versions: koshian, which is very fine and smooth, and tsubuan, a chunky version where some beans are left whole. I am partial to tsubuan for the texture, but also because it is less work to make as you don't need to separate the skins.

To make this smooth for koshian anko, simply add in the extra step of blending the beans fully in a food processor before putting back in the pan with the sugar and salt and passing through a fine-mesh sieve for the smoothest result. I make batches of it at a time and simply freeze what I'm not using immediately, for a rainy day.

234

METHOD

Rinse and drain the beans. Because they are so small, there is no need to soak them. Place in a pan with the water and bring to a gentle simmer, then cover and cook for 1 hour, or until the beans are so soft they can be easily squashed. Check occasionally to see if you need to top up with any water to keep the beans just covered.

Strain the beans (reserve the water if you are planning on making Zenzai, page 240). Place the beans back into the pan, pour over the sugar and salt and heat over a low–medium heat. Adding sugar makes the beans release water, so you should see that as the beans warm up they will soon be floating in liquid. Once they are floating, for tsubuan, blend the beans with an immersion (stick) blender, leaving about a third of the beans whole. For koshian, you can blend completely, then – to make it even smoother – pass through a fine-mesh sieve.

Continue to cook over a medium heat, stirring frequently so the mixture does not burn (be careful as it will splutter if given the chance), until you can draw a line in the bottom of the pan and it holds for a second or so. Remove from the heat and let the anko cool completely.

Use in your favourite recipe, enjoy by the spoonful or store for later use (it will keep in the freezer for up to 3 months, or in the fridge for up to 4 days).

INGREDIENTS

250 g (9 oz) dried red adzuki beans
1 litre (4 cups) water
220-250 g (1 generous cup) sugar
¼ teaspoon salt

甘

Red Bean Buns

あ
ん
パ
ン

One of my favourite snacks of all time is this perfectly simple, fluffy bun with a sweet filling of anko (red bean paste). These were one of the very early experiments with Western food in Japan and can be traced back to the Kimuraya bakery in Ginza, which opened in 1869. The Japanese were still not used to eating bread, but Yasubei Kimura, a samurai turned baker, knew that he needed to offer something that would be appreciated by the Japanese palate. Taking his cue from sakamanju, anko-filled steamed buns, Kimura invented a rice starter called sakadane, which is made with cooked rice, koji rice malt and water, to mimic European sourdough for a soft sweet bread that the Japanese would like and, in 1875, anpan was born. The Emperor himself was a fan. Kimuraya bakery still use the exact same recipe with sakadane sourdough, as the company's president, Mimiko Kimura, is determined to preserve the traditions of her ancestors.

For these buns, I turn to my milk bread dough for shokupan. You can follow the same recipe up to the shaping part. It makes a small batch because there is nothing like biting into a pillowy soft anpan while it is still warm. But you could easily double this and share them around, or freeze them for later.

Cont. >

235

い物

METHOD

Things to prepare in advance: Make the anko ahead of time and mix the yudane for the shokupan the night (or several hours at least) before starting the dough.

The next day, make the shokupan dough according to the recipe on page 221 and follow the instructions up until the shaping of the dough. After letting the dough rise to double the volume, divide it into 8 balls, roughly 75–80 g (2¾ oz) each. Try to divide the dough in as few cuts as possible, then gently roll the dough into perfect balls. I like to use a 'pinch and pull method', which I learned from cookbook author Kristina Cho, where you flatten them a little, then gently pull the edges of the dough in towards the centre and pinch to gather. Turn upside-down so you have the seam underneath and use your cupped hand over the top to gently roll the dough, pulling it towards you as you roll, then pull, roll and pull, to form a nice, taut, round bun. The seam should stay on the bottom. You can use the palm of your hand or your work surface for this action, in either case you need a bit of traction for that taut surface – for lovely buns you want to create some tension in the dough to hold that shape. Place a clean dish towel over the top and leave to rest for 10–15 minutes.

Divide the anko into 8 balls about the size of a walnut (roughly 30 g/1 oz each) and roll into neat balls. Damp hands help if it is sticky. It's helpful to have this ready in advance so you don't get anko all over your lovely dough.

Flatten the balls of dough to more or less the size of your palm and pinch the edges so they are a bit thinner. Place a ball of anko into the middle of the dough, bring the edges together around it and pinch closed. Turn over and, with your cupped hand over the top, roll gently into a nice shape as before. Place on a baking tray and leave to rise for 30–60 minutes, or until well puffed.

Preheat the oven to 180°C (350°F/gas 4).

Brush the dough balls with the beaten egg using a pastry brush and add a small sprinkle of sesame seeds to the centre of the bun. Bake for 15 minutes, or until deep golden brown and springy.

VARIATIONS

There are endless variations of anpan found in Japan, some of my favourites are seasonal specialties, like a sweet kabocha pumpkin (winter squash) or kurian (chestnut paste, page 248) filling. Custard or jam are popular, too.

INGREDIENTS

240 g (about 1 cup) Anko (page 234)
1 batch of Shokupan dough (page 221)
1 egg, beaten
black sesame seeds, to decorate

い物

Red Bean and Kanten Jelly Dessert

SERVES 4

あ
ん
み
つ

INGREDIENTS
200 g (about ¾ cup) Anko (page 234)
any seasonal fruit: for example,
  cherries, watermelon, peaches,
  in small pieces

KANTEN JELLY
250 ml (1 cup) water
2 teaspoons kanten or agar agar powder
2 tablespoons sugar
squeeze of lemon juice or 1 teaspoon
  powdered matcha (optional)

KUROMITSU SYRUP
50 g (¼ cup) black sugar (see opposite)
  (try muscovado/brown sugar
  if you can't get it)
2 tablespoons water

OPTIONAL ADDITIONS
ice cream (maybe matcha-flavoured
  or the Hojicha ice cream, page 232)
Dango (see page 240)
kinako (roasted soybean powder),
  for dusting on top

This is a charmingly old-fashioned Japanese dessert that I love to eat on a warm afternoon as a refreshing pick-me-up. Like Anpan (page 235), anmitsu was born almost a century ago in a shop in Tokyo's Ginza district, Ginza Wakamatsu, which is also a cafe specialising in sweet dishes. The shop's house-made anko was added to the top of mitsumame, a sweet dish of kanten jelly and fruit, and it became anmitsu.

Today, there are countless variations of this melange of little preparations and that is part of the beauty of this dish and the thing I find endlessly exciting when I see anmitsu on offer – it is presented differently every time you see it. Served in a bowl, you will generally find the original ingredients of mitsumame: kanten jelly (cubes of hard-set seaweed-jelly), boiled sweet mame peas, along with colourful, fresh or preserved seasonal fruit (popular old-school preserved fruits include tinned mandarin segments and maraschino cherries), shiratama dango (small, plain mochi rice balls) and kuromitsu on the side (a syrup of Okinawan black sugar). The kanten jelly might be flavoured with green tea, coffee, fruit juice, your favourite kind of milk or simply translucent glistening cubes of water and sugar. You often see a variation called cream anmitsu, which includes a scoop of ice cream on top, an excellent addition in the summer to this already refreshing, unique dessert that just happens to be made of seaweed, rice, fruit and beans.

Use any seasonal fruit, such as cherries, watermelon balls, peach cut into wedges, strawberries, bananas, mandarin segments, apple wedges, or tinned fruit if these are not in season, particularly cherries, peaches, pineapple or mandarins. The more colour, the better. If you want to add the dango balls, which are very easy to make, see the Zenzai recipe (page 240) for how to prepare them. All of these elements can be prepared ahead of time, but be sure to assemble just before you want to serve the anmitsu for ultimate freshness.

METHOD

For the kanten jelly, heat the measured water with the kanten powder and sugar. If you want to flavour it with either some lemon juice or matcha tea, stir this through too. Bring to a simmer and cook for 1–2 minutes. Remove from the heat and pour into a small container, tray or pan (an 11 cm × 21 cm/ 4¼ in × 8¼ in loaf pan, if it has a smooth surface, is ideal). Let the jelly cool at room temperature to set. When set, slice into cubes about 1.5 cm (½ in) wide.

For the syrup, simply heat the sugar with the water until the sugar is dissolved and the syrup has slightly thickened, 2 minutes or so.

To assemble the anmitsu, place a heaped tablespoon of anko in each of four dessert bowls, arrange the kanten jelly cubes around the anko, then distribute the pieces of fruit evenly. Serve immediately, with the syrup to pour over the top of each to your liking.

Black sugar has been made in Okinawa for four centuries. Pure sugar cane juice is boiled down until it is very, very dark and, when hard, it is then broken up into chunks or blocks, which is how you find it sold. It has a rich, caramel molasses-like flavour and is lovely in desserts as a syrup, in cakes, biscuits and milky tea, or as a powdered sugar (you just crush it between your fingers and it becomes a clumpy powder) to decorate desserts with, too. As it is less much refined than white or brown sugar, it retains many minerals and it is particularly rich in potassium and iron. A hot tea made with fresh ginger sweetened with black sugar is commonly made for women during their periods as an iron supplement or as a pick-me-up when you have a cold or general fatigue.

239

い物

Red Bean Soup
SERVES 4

ぜ
ん
ざ
い

There is nothing more comforting on a winter's day than warm, sweet red bean soup with dango (small, plain mochi rice balls). For me, it's even better than hot chocolate with whipped cream. I just feel nourished in every sense of the word when I eat this, it is pure comfort food. I will usually make this whenever I make a batch of anko, as the beans are already hot from being boiled – I admit, I love it so much I can't even resist it when I make anko in warm weather, but I always have Obaachan's words ringing in my ears when I eat warming mochi in soup: 'it will keep you warm all day long'.

Note that Japanese shiratamako rice flour is a glutinous rice flour sold in clumps rather than a smooth powder. You could replace it with mochiko rice flour instead, but be sure to use a Japanese rice flour and not another kind for these mochi. You could also use store-bought kirimochi, which are dried, and in this case, I would grill or toast them – just break up 2 kirimochi blocks into 8 pieces (they are scored to make breaking easy, it's bad luck to cut them) and heat them on a dry frying pan (skillet) or in a toaster oven until they are puffed and golden brown on both sides.

240

METHOD

Make the anko recipe as on page 234. I personally enjoy a chunkier tsubuan anko for this, blending only about halfway, but you can blend all the way for a smoother soup. Add enough of the reserved bean water to make a lovely thick soup, but slightly thinner than porridge or oatmeal. You may not need it all – if you have any leftovers you can freeze this like anko.

Make the dango mochi balls by placing the shiratamako flour in a bowl and adding the water. Knead until you have a smooth, bouncy, if somewhat chalky dough – it reminds me of air drying clay. If it is a bit crumbly, add some water to your hands and knead again until just right. Roll into roughly 8 walnut-sized balls and, with your thumb, make a little indentation in the centre of each. Boil them for 2 minutes, then drain (note, if you are making this ahead of time and not using the dango immediately, keep them in a bowl of cool water).

Ladle the hot red bean soup into bowls, place the dango inside and serve.

INGREDIENTS
1 batch of Anko (page 234)

DANGO
50 g (⅓ cup) shiratamako or mochiko rice flour
2 tablespoons water

甘

い物

甘

Strawberry Mochi

MAKES 6

い
ち
ご
大
福

Strawberry daifuku (meaning literally 'great luck') are made of a small round mochi filled with anko and a whole fresh strawberry. They have been popular since the 1980s and are a very special treat when strawberries are in season – I loved these as a child. The strawberries are usually enclosed entirely inside the mochi but I think this version, with the strawberry nestled on top, is so eye-catching. I also love the simplest version of mochi – rice mochi hiding an anko filling – and with this recipe you can choose to leave them that way, or score them on top and add the strawberry.

243

METHOD

Combine the rice flour with the water and sugar in a small, heatproof bowl. Cook it in a steamer, simply letting the steam gently cook the dough, checking 2–3 times and mixing with a wet spatula as needed for 12–15 minutes, or until the dough becomes thick with a completely translucent appearance. You can also microwave it in a similar way, checking for it to become translucent, and mixing 2–3 times in between.

Prepare a chopping board or tray dusted liberally with the potato starch.

Divide the anko into 6 balls, about 25 g (1 oz) each, roughly the size of a large cherry. If it is too sticky, wet your hands to help make nice smooth balls. Set them aside.

Tip the mochi dough onto the top of the potato starch and use a dough scraper or sharp knife to cut the dough into 6 even pieces. Dust with more potato starch, then roll one piece out to a thin circle, about 1–2 mm (1/16 in) thick, with a well-dusted rolling pin. You can also shape by hand, stretching the dough like a miniature pizza. Place a ball of anko in the middle of the dough and gather up all the edges, pinching to seal. Turn the mochi upside-down so the seam is facing down. Continue in the same way to make the rest.

With a sharp knife, cut a slit in the top of each daifuku and push a strawberry inside. These should be enjoyed immediately with a cup of green tea. Do not refrigerate mochi as they will become unpleasantly hard.

INGREDIENTS

90 g (½ cup) shiratamako rice flour
125 ml (½ cup) water
1 tablespoon sugar
1 tablespoon potato starch,
   or as needed
150 g (about ½ cup) smooth (koshian)
   Anko (page 234)
6 whole, not too large strawberries, hulled

い物

Rice Balls with Red Bean Paste

MAKES 12

おはぎ

These are homely rice balls made with sticky rice and anko to celebrate the autumn (fall) equinox and harvest (autumn time is rice harvest time), as ohagi vaguely resemble bush clover, a plant called hagi in Japanese that is in full bloom in autumn. The equinox is also a special time for a Buddhist practice called ohigan, where respects are paid to ancestors, and ohagi are traditional sweets to offer for this. Some people would use only glutinous rice in this, but this mixture of glutinous and regular short-grain rice was something I was shown in Nagano by a wonderful local cook called Ayumi, who prepared these mochi with a paste made from egoma (perilla seeds) and I loved the texture. My obaachan made delicious ohagi, where she mixed the sticky rice with millet, barley and buckwheat for a nutty flavour and texture – just use an even mix of both rices and these grains and cook as you would below.

METHOD

Combine the glutinous and regular rice in a saucepan and wash two or three times to remove some of the excess starch. Drain and cover with the measured water and bring to the boil. Cover, reduce the heat to the lowest setting and let it simmer until the rice is tender, about 15–17 minutes. Keep covered and let it steam off the heat for a further 10 minutes.

Now you need to pound the rice (like the rabbit in the moon, as Japanese folklore goes), you can use a pestle or something similar to partially pound it so you have a sticky mass.

Dip your hands in a bowl of salted water and roll the rice into 12 small balls about the size of walnuts in their shells (30 g/1 oz, or so). Shape them slightly into an oval/cylindrical shape and set aside.

Taking 60 g (¼ cup) portions of anko at a time, flatten the anko in the palm of your hand (again, wet hands helps the anko not to stick). Place a rice ball in the middle and wrap the anko around it to entirely enclose the rice. Place on a plate and continue with the rest.

Like mochi, ohagi are best on the day they are made, or at most kept cool for the next day, but don't place in the fridge as it ruins the texture. You can also share these around with your neighbours as a symbol of friendship and to ward off misfortune, a tradition that dates to the Edo period.

INGREDIENTS

70 g (⅓ cup) glutinous short-grain rice
70 g (⅓ cup) Japanese short-grain rice
250 ml (1 cup) water
salt
1 batch of chunky (tsubuan), thick Anko (page 234)

VARIATIONS

There is a spring equinox version of these too that are called botamochi. They are essentially the same, but inside-out – anko inside and pounded rice outside. Other regional variations are found where, for example, adzuki beans were not produced: kinako (roasted soybean powder) is the coating, or sweet, ground black sesame seeds.

244

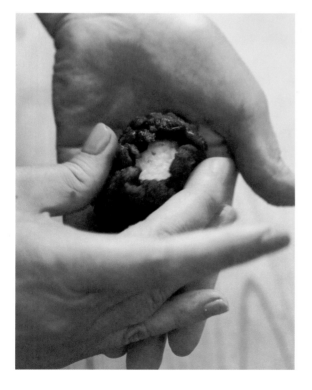

Chestnut-Filled Dorayaki Pancakes

MAKES 5

どら焼き

This delicious snack was born over a century ago in a shop called Usagiya in Tokyo's Ueno district, a favourite area of mine for its wonderful street food, sweets and lively markets. Dorayaki are made with the batter of a beloved Japanese cake, kasutera (or castella, a sponge-like cake adopted from the Portuguese). Honey (and often mirin) usually feature in this cake batter, which lends the outside of the cake, as well as these pancakes, a characteristic deep, dark brown colouring and a great aroma. They are usually filled with anko, but one autumn (fall), when I couldn't get to my local Asian grocer in Florence, I decided to replicate anko with chestnuts, which are a staple autumnal food in Italy. The chestnut cream has the same texture and all the familiarity of the traditional anko – and chestnuts are a much-loved autumn food in mountainous Japan, too, where the paste is called kurian.

You can use store-bought chestnut jam if you like, or even do this with the classic anko filling. This method of making the chestnut cream at home (inspired by the River Cottage) cuts out a chunk of the usual cooking time of the chestnuts by removing the skins after just a few minutes.

Cont. >

247

METHOD

For the kurian, with a sharp knife cut a slit in one side of each chestnut (in Italy, there are chestnut cutting tools that do just this without any danger of cutting your hand open; do be careful). Bring a large saucepan of water to the boil and blanch the chestnuts for about 2 minutes. Turn off the heat. Working on a handful of chestnuts at a time, remove from the water and while they are warm, peel off the skins (there are two layers, the shell and the skin). It can be fiddly and this is best done in a team, so get someone on board to help who will be paid in dorayaki.

Place the chestnuts back in the saucepan and fill with fresh water to cover. Bring to the boil and simmer until tender, about 20 minutes. If any foam rises to the surface, skim it off. With a slotted spoon, remove the chestnuts to a food processor and blend, adding some of the chestnut cooking water as needed to make a thick, smooth puree. Put the puree back in the (empty) pan along with the sugar. Stir and bring to a simmer over a low heat and cook until the sugar is dissolved (watch out, it will splutter a bit), about 5 minutes. This should make about double what you need for this recipe, but an extra jar of chestnut cream is not a bad thing. You can use it in place of the anko in any of the recipes in this chapter. If you put it in a sterilised jar and seal it, it should keep for 6 months.

For the dorayaki, use a whisk to beat the eggs in a jug with the sugar and honey until frothy and combined. Fold through the flour, cornflour and baking powder and let the mixture rest for 10 minutes.

Lightly grease a wide, non-stick frying pan (skillet) with vegetable oil, ensuring to remove any excess oil with some kitchen paper. Heat gently over a low heat.

Stir the water into the batter until the mixture is smooth. Pour some batter into the pan to make pancakes of 8–9 cm (3–3½ in) in diameter. Repeat to make 2 or 3 pancakes (this will depend on the size of your pan). Cook until you begin to see a bubble or two appear on the surface of the pancakes. With a spatula, carefully lift the pancakes and flip over. The surface should be an even, deep brown colour. Cook for a further minute, but not much longer, then remove the pancakes as they are ready to a plate. Keep the pancakes covered while you cook the rest so that they remain nice and soft for sandwiching. You will make 10 pancakes in total.

You'll find that the pancakes have a definite 'inside' and an 'outside' shape – reminiscent of a gong (*dora* actually means 'gong' in Japanese). Divide the kurian among four of the pancakes (on the 'inside'), then top with another pancake. These are delicious served immediately when still warm, or they can be served cold, but they are best on the day they are made.

Keep any uneaten dorayaki wrapped well or in an airtight container in the fridge, then gently warm them before eating to soften them again.

INGREDIENTS

KURIAN (CHESTNUT CREAM)
500 g (1 lb 2 oz) fresh chestnuts
180 g (¾ cup) sugar

DORAYAKI PANCAKES
2 eggs
50 g (¼ cup) sugar
1½ tablespoons honey
80 g (½ cup) plain (all-purpose) flour, sifted
1 tablespoon cornflour (corn starch), sifted
½ teaspoon baking powder
vegetable oil, for greasing
2 tablespoons water
250 g (scant 1 cup) kurian (or store-bought chestnut jam, or Anko, page 234)

い物

Arrowroot Mochi

SERVES 4

わ
ら
び
餅

250

INGREDIENTS

1 teaspoon matcha (green tea powder, see note)

35 g (⅓ cup) tapioca starch, sifted
1 tablespoon sugar
250 ml (1 cup) water
2 tablespoons kinako (roasted soybean powder), or as needed
Kuromitsu syrup (page 238), to serve

NOTE

Matcha powder has different grades and these grades correspond to different colours and prices. Matcha powder is separated into ceremonial-grade tea, the highest you can find, which makes a thick, very special, intense, vibrant green tea. Then you have culinary-grade matcha with a bright matcha colour, and you have ingredient-grade, which is the lowest grade and has a slightly yellower or olive green colour. If you want a very nice, bright green colour, you could go for the culinary-grade matcha, but be aware it's not suitable for making tea with – or just splurge on a ceremonial-grade one that you can also use for making cups of tea.

Made with tapioca starch (arrowroot), these deliciously chewy, refreshing mochi are so easy to prepare and perfect on a summer afternoon. Traditionally, they were made with the starch from the roots of bracken (warabi), a type of fern, but this starch is hard to get and very expensive, so often warabimochi is now made with tapioca or sweet potato starch. It has two of my favourite accompaniments: kinako (roasted soybean powder) and kuromitsu (black sugar syrup). I added a third, matcha, which is another wonderful variation on its own, but because I wanted it all at once, I put both kinako and matcha on at the same time, which I so love and it is also a pretty presentation.

Please note that this mochi is really very sticky! The kinako is important as it will coat the sticky mochi so that it is manageable. The matcha is just there for colour and flavour; it does not help hold the mochi together or make it less sticky, as the kinako does. You can leave out the matcha if you like, but the kinako is a must. If you find you need to dust more than the recipe calls for, go for it.

You could also turn this into a dessert bowl similar to Anmitsu (page 238) by adding some Anko (page 234) and Hojicha ice cream (page 232).

METHOD

Prepare a board or a tray with a good dusting of half the kinako, followed by a light dusting of matcha powder (the layering is important, don't mix).

Combine the tapioca starch and sugar with the measured water in a small saucepan. Whisk over a medium heat, you will see it turn quite quickly from milky white to a thick, translucent and sticky paste.

Pour the mochi paste onto the tray of matcha powder, dust over a little more matcha and let it cool. The matcha will seep into the mochi, giving it some colour. Now dust the rest of the kinako over the top of it, cut with a sharp knife into 2.5 cm (1 in) squares, carefully separate and dust more kinako over the top to coat them on all sides.

Serve with a drizzle of kuromitsu syrup poured over the top with a glass of iced hojicha (roasted green tea).

Any leftovers can be refrigerated for 1–2 days.

い物

甘

Kanten Fruit Jelly Cups

MAKES 6 JELLIES

寒
天
ゼ
リ
ー

253

These fun, simple fruit cups are a hit with children and adults alike and might even be served as breakfast – they are so fast to make because kanten sets at room temperature, unlike jelly made from gelatin. Kanten is a plant-based gelatin made from a type of red algae called tengusa and was discovered by accident in the mid-1600s. The word agar agar is often used as a synonym for kanten, but in Japan they are considered two different ingredients as they actually come from different varieties of seaweed.

You can make these all plain or add a layer of milk kanten – or replace the milk with a fruit juice of choice, blackcurrant would be pretty, for example. The fruit in the recipe here is just an idea, choose seasonal, colourful favourite fruits – you can even do this with just one type of fruit, which makes quite a stunning-looking jelly, too.

A silicon muffin pan is helpful for this as it is easy to turn them out, but you can also use a tray shape or even a cake tin where you cut these into slices. Alternatively, pour into glasses or ramekins where you can serve as is, without turning them out. In this case, make them upside-down with the milk layer first and then the fruit and plain kanten layer.

METHOD

Distribute the fruit evenly among six holes of a silicon muffin pan.

To make the plain kanten, combine the kanten powder with the sugar and measured water in a small saucepan. Simmer for 1–2 minutes, stirring to dissolve the sugar. Let cool slightly (not too long as it will start to set!), then pour over the fruit in the cups. Place in the fridge to help them set, it should only take 10 minutes.

In the meantime, make the milk kanten. Combine the kanten powder with the sugar, milk and measured water in the saucepan and simmer for 1–2 minutes, stirring to dissolve the sugar, and once this has cooled ever so slightly, pour it over the top of the set kanten for a milk layer. Chill in the fridge for 10 minutes to set, then turn them out onto small plates and serve.

INGREDIENTS

1 punnet of blueberries
6 cherries or strawberries, halved
1 nectarine, kiwifruit, nashi pear
  or mandarin, cut into small pieces

PLAIN KANTEN
2 g (⅛ oz) kanten powder (or agar agar)
2 teaspoons sugar
250 ml (1 cup) water

MILK KANTEN
2 g (⅛ oz) kanten powder (or agar agar)
2 teaspoons sugar
160 ml (⅔ cup) milk
80 ml (⅓ cup) water

Matcha Tiramisu

SERVES 4–6

抹茶ティラミス

I am generally not one for mashing up two such important cultural icons, but I have to admit that this is really good – the sweetness of the mascarpone cream and the bitterness of matcha are just a match made in heaven – to the point that matcha tiramisu has become a classic in its own right. I love this in a pretty bowl or you can do individual portions in glasses or ramekins.

254

INGREDIENTS

3 eggs, separated
70 g (scant ⅓ cup) sugar
300 g (1¼ cups) mascarpone
2 teaspoons matcha (green tea
   powder, see note on page 250),
   plus extra for dusting
125 ml (½ cup) water
100 g (3½ oz) savoiardi biscuits
   (sponge fingers)

METHOD

To make the mascarpone cream, whisk the egg whites (make sure you use a very clean bowl – glass or metal is best – and very clean beaters to quickly get beautifully stiff whites) until you have soft, fluffy peaks that hold their shape.

In a separate bowl, whip the egg yolks with the sugar until you have a creamy and pale mixture. Whip in the mascarpone, 1½ teaspoons of the matcha, and finally fold in the egg whites. Set aside (if not using immediately, store covered in the fridge).

Mix the remaining ½ teaspoon of matcha in the measured water. Quickly dip one side (and one side only) of a savoiardi biscuit into the matcha and layer, matcha-side up, in a baking dish or large bowl. Repeat until you have a nice, tight layer that covers the base of the dish. Cover the savoiardi with a thick layer of matcha cream. Repeat to make another layer of savoiardi dipped in matcha, and finish with another layer of cream.

Cover and chill in the fridge overnight (or for at least 4 hours, if you are in a hurry, but the longer the better). When ready to serve, dust with more matcha powder.

小物

Kinako and Chestnut Cake

SERVES 8

きな粉と栗のケーキ

Kinako is one of my favourite flavours in Japanese sweets – dusted over the top of Warabimochi (page 250) or Anmitsu (page 238), for example, or topping dango or mochi. It is a roasted soybean powder and has a naturally sweet and nutty flavour. It is a 500-year-old ingredient in Japanese cuisine, cited in cookbooks from the Muromachi period. Because of its nutty flavour, it goes well with other nutty things and I couldn't help but pair this pound cake with some freshly boiled chestnuts that I had just made for Kurian (page 247) – in fact you can reference that recipe for cooking chestnuts for this one. You could also use pre-cooked chestnuts for this, which are usually found in the dried fruit section of the supermarket, or kuromame, which are black beans cooked in soy sauce and sugar, a special dish for New Year, which you can buy pre-made and are becoming easier to find (I've even found them in Milan).

256

INGREDIENTS

250 g (9 oz) butter, at room
   temperature, plus extra for greasing
150 g (⅔ cups) sugar
2 tablespoons Okinawan black sugar
   (or brown sugar)
4 eggs, at room temperature
200 g (1⅓ cups) plain (all-purpose) flour
50 g (generous ½ cup) kinako (roasted
   soybean powder)
10–12 whole boiled or roasted
   chestnuts, peeled

NOTE

The black sugar helps give it a nice caramel colour, as does the kinako. You can use brown sugar instead. To bring your eggs and butter to room temperature, let them sit on the work surface for at least 30 minutes. I like to chop the butter first to help it along. If you forget to do this (I am guilty of this all the time), do not just use them cold – place the eggs in a stainless-steel bowl full of very warm water for 5 minutes.

METHOD

Preheat the oven to 170°C (340°F). Grease and line a loaf tin. Loaf tins can vary in size, so feel free to use what you have, but I like to use a slightly shorter-than-usual loaf tin (20 cm × 11 cm × 7 cm/8 in × 4¼ in × 2¾ in), as I get taller cakes this way.

Cream the butter and sugars together until pale and creamy. Add the eggs, one by one, beating well after each addition. Once all the eggs are in, beat continuously until very, very pale and fluffy. This takes about 7 minutes with electric beaters. There are no other rising agents in this cake, so the whipping is important. Fold in the flour and kinako carefully until just combined.

Pour half of the batter into the prepared loaf tin, drop in about half of the chestnuts, then add some more batter to cover the chestnuts. Dot over the remaining chestnuts, then cover completely with the rest of the batter.

Bake for 1 hour, or until golden on top and a wooden skewer inserted into the middle comes out clean.

甘

Haruko's Matcha Almond Cookies

MAKES ABOUT 36 SMALL COOKIES

晴子さんの抹茶クッキー

258

My mother's best friend, Haruko (who, like my mother, was married to an Australian), was a great cookie baker and made exceptional Christmas cookie tins. One day she asked my mother and me if we could make the cookies she bakes every Christmas to give to friends and family, as she was feeling too weak to do them – she was battling cancer.

She gave us some batches of cookie dough that she had already prepared, along with her recipes for others that still needed making, with plenty of instructions and drawings of the right shape and icing for each, and we spent days, working late into the night, baking chocolate almond cookies, pecan sandies, gingerbread, banana and lemon cookies, and soft, buttery matcha cookies, all of them rolled out and cut into delicate little shapes like cherry blossoms and miniature Christmas trees, then popped into old-fashioned cookie tins to give to her friends and family. It was a complete labour of love for me and my mother. And it was also Haruko's last Christmas.

These melt-in-the-mouth cookies are just the kind of thing Obaachan would have served with a proper cup of tea in one of the beautiful Wedgwood teacups from her precious collection. I like these with quite a lot of matcha, but you can use a little less for paler cookies and a more delicate flavour.

INGREDIENTS

125 g (4½ oz) unsalted butter, softened
45 g (⅓ cup) icing (confectioner's) sugar
150 g (1 cup) plain (all-purpose) flour, plus extra for dusting
50 g (½ cup) finely ground almond meal
4 teaspoons matcha (green tea powder, see note on page 250), plus extra for dusting
½ teaspoon natural vanilla extract

FOR THE ICING

2 teaspoons egg white or water
4 tablespoons icing (confectioner's) sugar

NOTE

If using American cups, you will need to add an extra ¼ cup flour. If in doubt, weigh your ingredients!

METHOD

Beat the butter until creamy and smooth, then add the other ingredients and combine to make a smooth, soft dough. Wrap in cling film (plastic wrap) and chill in the fridge for 30 minutes if it is a bit too soft.

Roll out the dough on a lightly floured surface to about 8 mm (⅜ in) thick. Cut out shapes with a cookie cutter and place on a baking tray lined with baking paper. If you are making these on a warm day, it is a good idea to put them in the fridge to chill for at least 20 minutes before baking.

Preheat the oven to 160°C (320°F/gas 3).

Bake for 12–13 minutes, or until the cookies are still pale but dry to the touch. Remove from the oven and leave to cool for 5 minutes on the baking tray before moving to a wire rack.

In the meantime, make the icing by mixing the egg white or water, little by little, into the icing sugar until you have a thick but smooth paste.

Ice the cookies as you wish and dust over some matcha powder. Let them set, then store in an airtight container. I love these the next day, as they soften more and almost melt in the mouth.

い物

FURTHER READING

参考資料

These are some of the sources in English that I highly recommend for those looking to dig deeper into Japanese home cooking; I have found them inspiring and helpful. There are cookbooks, but also websites, a memoir, an essay first published in the 1930s, an excellent dictionary and even a novel, *An*, or *Sweet Red Bean* as it's known in its translation, which was also made into a film (and if we are going to add films here I would include the cult classic *Tampopo*, especially for the omuraisu scene, and the irresistible series of Tokyo stories and food, *Midnight Diner*).

Katherine Tamiko Arguile's *Meshi: A Personal History of Japanese Food*, Affirm Press, 2022

Nami Chen's website *Just One Cookbook*, justonecookbook.com

The Youtube channel *Cooking with Dog*, cookingwithdog.com

Yuki Gomi's blog *Yuki's Kitchen*, yukiskitchen.com

Nancy Singleton Hachisu's *Japan: The Cookbook*, Phaidon Press Ltd, 2018

Yukio Hattori's *An Illustrated Guide to Japanese Cooking and Annual Events*, English translation by Toko Takao, Tankosha Publishing Co, 2017

Richard Hosking's *A Dictionary of Japanese Food: Ingredients and Culture*, Tuttle Publishing, 1996

Ishige Naomichi's *The History and Culture of Japanese Food*, Routledge, 2011

Harumi Kurihara's *Everyday Harumi*, Conran Octopus Ltd, 2009

Adam Liaw's *The Zen Kitchen*, Hachette Australia, 2016

Hiroko Liston's website *Hiroko's Recipes*, hirokoliston.com

Mayuko Matsumura's *Recipes of the World's Most Popular Japanese Dishes*, Ikeda Publishing Co, 2016

Maori Murota's *Tokyo: Cult Recipes*, Murdoch Books, 2015

Momoko Nakamura's website, momokonakamura.com

Yuto Omura's website *Sudachi Recipes*, sudachirecipes.com

Tadashi Ono and Harris Salat's *Japanese Soul Cooking: Ramen, Tonkatsu, Tempura and More from the Streets and Kitchens of Tokyo and Beyond*, Ten Speed Press, 2013

Sachiko Saeki's website *Kinome Japonica*, kinomekitchen.co.uk

Durian Sukegawa's *Sweet Bean Paste*, English translation by Alison Watts, One World, 2017

Jun'ichiro Tanizaki's *In Praise of Shadows*, English translation by Thomas J Harper and Edward G Seidensticker, Leete's Island Books, Bramford, 1977

Shizuo Tsuji's *Japanese Cooking: A Simple Art*, US edition, Kodansha USA Publishing, New York, 2011

Shihoko Ura's website *Chopstick Chronicles*, chopstickchronicles.com

Reiko Yamada Wagohan's *The ABCs of Japanese Cuisine*, English translation by Hibiki Mizuno, Pot Publishing, Tokyo, 2017

ACKNOWLEDGEMENTS

お
わ
り
に

Sitting in a cafe in Florence once with my friend and mentor, Tessa Kiros (whose cookbooks I read cover to cover long before I even dared dream of writing cookbooks), she said, 'Why don't you write a Japanese cookbook? Something of your heritage? I'd get that.' After chatting with Tessa, it dawned on me that the food that so many people know of as Japanese cooking comes from international restaurants, which is not the same thing that you experience at home with a Japanese parent or grandparent cooking for you. Japanese home cooking is far from intimidating, it's simple, fresh and surely worth sharing with others. So I must thank Tessa Kiros for not only planting the first seed, but because she also encouraged me to embrace my Japanese heritage.

As a half Japanese person who doesn't look at all Japanese, I have often felt like a fraud calling myself Japanese. So different did I look from my mother, with my green eyes and wavy hair, that people thought she was my nanny. I've carried a Japanese passport for most of my life but I had little other 'proof' of my Japanese-ness. My spoken Japanese is only what I picked up as a child; I can understand it quite a bit, but I read and write like a six-year-old. I couldn't communicate fully with my grandparents (though we never had problems understanding each other, especially at the table). I struggled to feel Japanese enough to be allowed to tell the story behind the food that I grew up with, the food I consider the most special in the world, even as I watched as plenty of non-Japanese people did. But inevitably the desire to create this book proved stronger than the fear of imposter syndrome and it has given me the courage to allow myself to connect to and express this half of my identity. The result is a love letter to the home cooking my heart and taste buds know best, Japanese home cooking.

When my first proposal was turned down (which made me doubt my Japanese-ness even more), I sat on the idea for another two years, waiting for the pandemic to pass so I could go back to Japan for some more inspiration to rewrite my proposal. But before that happened I had a chance to show it to Paul McNally at Smith Street Books, who was my very first publisher almost a decade ago at Hardie Grant. Paul — I can't thank you enough for believing in this proposal from the moment you saw it. Cheesy mochi forever.

261

I must also thank my wonderful editors Hannah Koelmeyer and Emily Preece-Morrison for their keen eye and patience and for helping make this book the best version it can be.

Thank you, too, to my dear friends Junko and Yuta Mizoguchi, who live just down the road from me in our little Tuscan town and have shared so much more with me than just good food. I would also like to thank Megan Dung and the team at Chino Tabi for organising a dream stay in Chino, Nagano, which appears in a number of the location photos in this book, and to extend a huge thank you to Kobayashi-san, who made tofu with us at his family tofu shop in Chino, Sennan Tofu.

Thank you to my family (especially my husband Marco) for all your support, as always — the Italian side, the Australian side and the Japanese side. I am so grateful.

This is unlike any of my previous books in so many ways. It's much more personal. Each and every recipe in this book is food that makes me nostalgic, that can bring me to tears, make me jump with joy or sedate me with comfort. I couldn't have written it without the help of my mother, Sumie, whose home cooking will forever be the best, for me. She kept her children always connected to Japan, making sure we visited my family every single year — I sometimes stayed for extended periods, attending preschool or staying for the whole summer. These annual visits continued until my grandparents passed away in my twenties, and they've grown less frequent since then. Things are not the same without them but cooking and eating the food that reminds me most of them keeps us connected.

Something I would really like to acknowledge here is the involvement of all the proud, talented Asian women who helped bring this cookbook to life.

Thanks to my mother and my grandmother's delicious cooking, I grew up with a passionate appreciation and curiosity for food, as well as a palate that will forever have a special preference for rice, fish, chestnuts, incredibly crunchy cucumbers, seaweed, sesame, mochi and soba. But I didn't learn to cook many Japanese dishes through them. For that I am indebted to the Japanese food writers who, like my mother, emigrated overseas and decided to write about their food in English. Often I would message my mother asking her for her recipe for a dish – but because she cooks by eye and doesn't really use recipes (the lemon and daikon pickles on page 52 are a perfect example), she would send me back a link for a similar recipe in English. For over a decade, I have cooked and read the blogs of Namiko Chen of *Just One Cookbook* in the US and Shihoko Ura of *Chopstick Chronicles* in Australia; later I also discovered Maori Murota who lives in Paris and Yuki Gomi who teaches Japanese cooking in London, also online (she first showed me how to make homemade miso and udon). Together with some cookbooks that I treasure (see page 260 for more), what they do has connected me to my Japanese heritage over the years.

I knew that somehow I had to get Evi O on board to design the book and I was thrilled when she accepted. Evi's work on other Japanese books, her aesthetics and brilliant brain turned this into exactly the kind of book I had hoped for – something that didn't feel intimidating, but that spoke of home and family.

Although I took most of the photographs in this book, I enlisted the help of Yuki Sugiura, a photographer I admire immensely – working with her was a dream. Thank you, Yuki, fellow anko-lover!

My sister, Hana Davies, a talented photographer with an incredible eye for detail, spent months editing all of my photographs and made them actually usable. We were able to visit Japan together too and she also is responsible for several photographs within these pages. It means so much to me that we made this together.

Although she may not be aware, Hetty McKinnon inspired and encouraged me to make this book first, through her beautiful independent publication, *Peddler Journal*, where I have often been given the chance to write about the food I grew up with before I had an outlet. And secondly, through her own book *To Asia, With Love*, which gave me the courage to believe it is possible to write something different, to write about the food I know with all my heart.

Another influential person for me is Momoko Nakamura, who teaches about the concept of Japanese microseasonality through journalling and how to connect to your Japanese ancestry.

I want to thank Yuki Kokubo for her beautiful, upcycled kimono fabrics that you can catch glimpses of in this book – my obaachan, who was a talented seamstress, would have loved these. And thank you Julie Newton for dropping in right in the middle of recipe testing and being a guinea pig and excellent hand model.

Last but not least, I had a small army of incredible recipe testers, home cooks from all over the world, who came on board and selected recipes to make for their families and supply feedback. I am so grateful: their work is one of the most important parts of making a cookbook for me as it gives me the confidence to put these recipes out into the world knowing they have been successfully shopped for, cooked and enjoyed in homes from Brooklyn to Rome to countryside Australia and beyond. Thank you from the bottom of my heart: Nathalie Boisard-Beudin, Gabrielle Schaffner, Sarah Slack, Yuko Naito, Xinyue Pan, Ilaria Falorsi, Amanda Cumming, Jessica Safirstein, Jacqueline Fuller, Lee Towle, Grace Chung, Racheli Herskowits, Christina Skavicus, Tiffany Zhou, Manon Koopman, Emma Jane Sekuless, Lisa Brown, Sally Frawley, Jun Merrett, Tamaron Jang Bertelli, Stephanie Whidden, Debra Austen, Teresa Mueller, Anne Bright, Sherri Billimoria, Karuna Luchmaya, Jeannie C, Diane Thompson, Kathy Yoshida, Lizzie and Sen Jayaprakasam, Daniela Walls, Suzanne Shier, Peggy Witter.

ありがとうございました!

ABOUT THE
AUTHOR

著者について

Emiko Davies is an award-winning food writer and photographer. Born in Australia to a Japanese mother and Australian father, she has spent most of her life living abroad: after an adolescence spent in China, she gained a Bachelor of Fine Art in the US and moved to Tuscany, which she has called home now for almost two decades. In late 2010, while living in Florence with her Tuscan sommelier husband, Marco Lami, she began writing a food blog, where she still documents regional recipes, travel guides and food stories. She has contributed to numerous publications, including *Financial Times*, *Gourmet Traveller*, *Food & Wine*, *Food52* and *Peddler Journal* and she writes a monthly recipe column inspired by historic cookbooks for Italy's leading newspaper, *Corriere della Sera*, who named her one of the 50 most powerful women in food in 2020. This is her sixth cookbook. She lives in the town of San Miniato, Tuscany, with her husband and their two Italian–Australian–Japanese children.

267

269

270

271

Published in 2023 by Smith Street Books
Naarm (Melbourne) | Australia
smithstreetbooks.com

ISBN: 978-1-9227-5452-3

Smith Street Books respectfully acknowledges the Wurundjeri People of the Kulin
Nation, who are the Traditional Owners of the land on which we work, and we pay
our respects to their Elders past and present.

Publisher: Paul McNally
Senior Editor: Hannah Koelmeyer
Editor: Emily Preece-Morrison
Photography: Emiko Davies, Hana Davies & Yuki Sugiura
Design and illustrations: Evi-O.Studio | Evi O.
Design assistant: Evi-O.Studio | Katherine Zhang
Food preparation and styling: Emiko Davies
Proofreader: Pam Dunne
Indexer: Helena Holmgren

Printed & bound in China by C&C Offset Printing Co., Ltd.

Book 279
10 9 8 7 6 5 4